AMERICAN ASSOCIATION OF COLLEGIATE REGISTRARS AND ADMISSIONS OFFICERS

AACRAO
1 9 1 0

2010 FERPA
Quick Guide

What You Need to Know About the
Family Educational Rights & Privacy Act

edited by LeRoy Rooker

Table of Contents

American Association of Collegiate
Registrars and Admissions Officers
One Dupont Circle, NW, Suite 520
Washington, DC 20036-1135

Tel: (202) 293-9161 | Fax: (202) 872-8857 | www.aacrao.org

For a complete listing of AACRAO publications, visit www.aacrao.org/publications/.

The American Association of Collegiate Registrars and Admissions Officers, founded in 1910, is a nonprofit, voluntary, professional association of more than 10,000 higher education administrators who represent more than 2,600 institutions and agencies in the United States and in twenty-eight countries around the world. The mission of the Association is to provide leadership in policy initiation, interpretation, and implementation in the global educational community. This is accomplished through the identification and promotion of standards and best practices in enrollment management, information technology, instructional management, and student services.

LIBRARY OF CONGRESS CATALOGING-IN-PUBLICATION DATA

The AACRAO 2010 FERPA quick guide : what you need to know about the Family
   Educational Rights & Privacy Act.

   p. cm.

   ISBN 978-1-57858-095-8

1.   United States. Family Educational Rights and Privacy Act.
2.   Student records—Law and legislation—United States.
3.   Privacy, Right of—United States.
4.   College registrars—United States—Handbooks, manuals, etc.
5.   College admission officers—United States—Handbooks, manuals, etc.

I.   American Association of Collegiate Registrars and Admissions Officers.
II. Title: 2010 FERPA quick guide.
III. Title: FERPA quick guide.

KF4156.5.A3281974A2 2010
342.7308'58—dc22
2010045214

Preface

The *FERPA Quick Guide* was written for higher education administrators entrusted with the task of storing, handling and releasing student records. It provides a basic overview of the *Family Educational Rights and Privacy Act of 1974*, as amended, the full text of its regulations, and a summary of the 2009 regulatory changes. In addition, this guide highlights how the Act applies to various school officials, including brief outlines of key terms and issues as well as commonly asked questions.

The *Quick Guide* is a useful introduction to FERPA. To obtain a more detailed analysis and application of the Act, as well as extensive FERPA training materials and case studies, refer to the *AACRAO 2010 FERPA Guide*. To order this and other professional development resources published by AACRAO, visit www.aacrao.org/publications/.

◇◇◇◇◇◇◇◇◇◇◇◇◇◇◇◇◇◇◇

CHAPTER ONE

Introduction

Under the *Family Educational Rights and Privacy Act* (hereafter referred to as The Act or FERPA), students are given three primary rights. They have the right to:

- Inspect and review their education records.
- Have some control over the disclosure of information from their education records.
- Seek to amend incorrect education records.

Educational institutions and agencies should conform to fair information practices. This means that persons who are subjects of data systems (*i.e.*, students at an institution) must:

- Be informed of the existence of such systems.
- Be apprised of what data about them is on record.
- Be given assurances that such data is used only for intended purposes.
- Be given the opportunity to request an amendment or correction to their records.
- Be certain that those responsible for data systems take reasonable precautions to prevent misuse of the data.
- Know that the institution will reasonably respond when an alleged misuse of, or access to, data is brought to the attention of those responsible for data systems.

Although The Act does not require it, those responsible for data systems are obliged to consider properly disposing of, or destroying, information when 1) the conditions under which that information was collected no longer exist and 2) there are no legal restrictions preventing such disposal.

Essence of the Act

FERPA deals specifically with the education records of students, affording them certain rights with respect to those records. For purposes of definition, education records are those records which are 1) directly related to a student and 2) maintained by an institution or a party acting for the institution.

FERPA gives students who reach the age of 18, or who attend a postsecondary institution, the right to inspect and review their own education records. Furthermore, students have other rights including the right to request amendment of records and to have some control over the disclosure of personally identifiable information from these records.

FERPA applies to all educational agencies and institutions that receive funding under most programs administered by the Secretary of Education (34 C.F.R. 99.1). Almost all postsecondary institutions, both public and private, generally receive such funding and must, therefore, comply with FERPA.

Institutions must annually notify students currently in attendance of their rights by any means that are likely to be read by students. The most common examples are found in the student handbook, catalog, or student newspaper. This notice also applies to any students pursuing education via distance education or any other non-traditional educational delivery processes. (*See* Appendix C, on page 81, for a sample of a model annual notification statement provided by the Family Policy Compliance Office.)

The regulations do not specify the means to be used for annually notifying students regarding their FERPA rights. Schools are not required by FERPA to notify former students of their FERPA rights. Although it is highly recommended that each institution publish its annual notification on its Web site, this method is only acceptable for fulfilling the annual notification requirement if all students are required to have personal computers or free and convenient access to computers that can access the institution's Web site.

If every enrolled student is given an institutional email address, schools may send their annual notification via email to their students.

Institutions may not disclose information contained in education records without the student's written consent except under conditions specified in The Act. An institution is not required to disclose information from a student's education records to the parents of dependent students but may exercise its discretion to do so. It is the responsibility of an institution to ensure that information is not improperly disclosed to the parents of students.

To Whose Records Does the Act Apply?

FERPA applies to the education records of persons who are, or have been, in attendance in postsecondary institutions, including students in cooperative and correspondence study programs and in any non-traditional educational delivery processes, such as distance learning.

FERPA does not apply to records of applicants for admission who are denied acceptance or, if accepted, do not attend an institution. Furthermore, rights are not given by FERPA to students enrolled in one component of an institution who seek to be admitted in another component of a school (*e.g.*, a student, admitted to one college within a university, but denied admission in another college, does not have any FERPA rights in the college which denied him/her admission).

To What Records Does the Act Apply?

The Act applies to all education records maintained by a postsecondary institution, or by a party acting for the institution, which are directly related to a student. Records containing a student's name, social security number or other personally identifiable information, in whatever medium, are covered by FERPA unless identified in one of The Act's excluded categories (*see* "Education Records," on page 17, for excluded categories).

To Which Institutions Does the Act Apply?

The Act applies to all institutions that receive funds administered by the Secretary of Education. This funding can either be in direct grants to the institution or to students attending the institution (financial aid). The Act applies to the entire institution even though only one component, *e.g.*, department or college, of the institution receives such funding.

Enforcement and Penalties

Responsibility for administering The Act has been assigned to the Family Policy Compliance Office within the Department of Education. This office reviews and investigates complaints, whether brought by the affected eligible student or otherwise brought to the attention of that office. When a violation has been found, FPCO attempts to bring about compliance through voluntary means, including any changes to the policies or practices of the institution. The penalty for noncompliance with FERPA can be withholding payments of Department of Education funds from the institution, issuing a cease and desist order, or terminating eligibility to receive funds; such actions generally will be taken only if compliance cannot be secured by voluntary means.

Conflict With State Law

FERPA may be more permissive than the privacy laws of some states. If a conflict exists between FERPA and a state or local law, and if an institution determines that it cannot comply with the requirements of The Act, it should advise the Family Policy Compliance Office, U.S. Department of Education, 400 Maryland Avenue, SW, Washington, D.C. 20202–5901; phone: (202) 260–3887; fax: (202) 260–9001, within 45 days of that determination, giving the text and legal citation of the conflicting law. These guidelines, therefore, should not be interpreted to reduce the stringency of such state laws. They counsel common sense, good judgment, perspective, and integrity for compliance by postsecondary institutions in the implementation of The Act.

Several challenges to FERPA were made during the 1990s based on various states' open records/meetings laws. In general, sunshine/open records laws do not supersede FERPA; thus, schools must continue to comply with FERPA. Any perceived conflict between a state open records law and FERPA should be brought to the attention of the Family Policy Compliance Office.

The "Musts" and "Mays" in FERPA

Throughout The Act, the words "may" and "must" are used. These words are usually used in connection with sections of The Act that either permit or require an institution to perform an action to comply with FERPA. In the former case, the institution has control over a decision; in other words, it *may* do something. In the latter case, the institution has no choice; in other words, it *must* do something.

There are many "mays" and a few "musts" in FERPA. The reader should be aware of these words and not consider an institution legally obliged to release education record information when FERPA actually states that the institution *may* release education record information. For example, FERPA states that each institution may identify certain items as directory information; however, this is an institutional decision. By deciding not to identify any items as directory information, the institution would be making a decision that could have a major administrative impact on all offices. For example, consider the challenges of producing a commencement program if the names of all the graduates and their degrees were not identified as directory information.

Note that the "may" under FERPA could become a "must" for public institutions in a state where the Open Records Law requires release of information that FERPA permits to be released, or under other legislation that might require all institutions in that state to release information releasable under FERPA.

◇◇◇◇◇◇◇◇◇◇◇◇◇◇◇◇

CHAPTER TWO

FERPA At-A-Glance

If you are looking for a summary of what FERPA is all about, the following statements capture its essence:

◆ Students at postsecondary institutions must be permitted to inspect and review their education records.

◆ School officials may not disclose personally identifiable information from a student's education record, without written permission, unless such a disclosure is permitted by one of the FERPA signed-consent exceptions.

◆ Institutions are responsible for ensuring that all of their school officials comply with FERPA.

If you are looking for a more detailed summary of FERPA, the following will be helpful.

What is FERPA?

The *Family Educational Rights and Privacy Act of 1974*, as amended, sets forth requirements regarding the privacy of student records. This law applies to postsecondary institutions as well as K–12 schools.

FERPA governs:

◆ The disclosure of education records maintained by an educational institution; and

◆ Access to these records.

Who *must* comply with FERPA?

Any educational institution (school or other entity that provides educational services and is attended by students) or educational agency (entity that administers schools directly linked to it) that receive funds under any program administered by the U.S. Secretary of Education.

What does FERPA require for colleges to be in compliance?

◆ Institutions must notify students annually of their FERPA rights *(see* Appendix C, "Model Notification of Rights under FERPA for Postsecondary Institutions," on page 81).

There is no specific method that schools must use to notify students—it is up to the institution. Notice must take a form that is "reasonably likely" to notify students. Recommended and most frequently used ways include: student bulletin, handbook or catalog; school or local newspaper; student registration packet; email notice of basic issues with a link to additional information.

◆ Ensure students' rights to inspect and review their education records.

◆ Ensure students' rights to request to amend their education records.

◆ Ensure students' rights to limit disclosure of personally identifiable information contained in education records.

◆ Notify third parties of the redisclosure prohibition of personally identifiable information (except under a few circumstances).

◆ Keep records of requests for and disclosures of student education records.

Who has FERPA rights at the postsecondary level?

◆ FERPA rights belong to the student at a postsecondary institution regardless of age.

◆ *Student* applies to all students—including continuing education students, students auditing a class, distance education students, and former students.

◆ *In attendance* can be defined by the institution, but it cannot be later than the day that the student first attends a class at the institution.

What FERPA rights are given to students?

◆ Right to inspect and review their education records.

◆ Right to request to amend their education records.

◆ Right to limit disclosure of "personally identifiable information" (information that would directly identify the student or make the student's identity easily traceable) known as *directory information.*

◆ Right to file a complaint with the Department of Education concerning an alleged failure by the institution to comply with FERPA.

What are education records under FERPA?

◆ Education records are defined as records that are:
  ▶ Directly related to a student, and
  ▶ Maintained by an educational agency or institution or by a party acting for the agency or institution, if certain conditions are met.

◆ Education records are not: sole possession records, law enforcement unit records, employment records, medical records, or post-attendance records.

To whom, and under what conditions, can colleges disclose personally identifiable information?

◆ Anyone, if the college has obtained the prior written consent of the student

◆ Anyone, in response to requests for directory information (Information that is generally not considered harmful or an invasion of privacy if disclosed)
  ▶ Institutions must identify those items it considers directory information and notify students.
  ▶ Institutions must inform students that they can withhold release of this information.

◆ Authorized representatives of the following government entities, if the disclosure is in connection with an audit or evaluation of federal or state supported education programs, or for the enforcement of or compliance with federal legal requirements that relate to those programs:
  ▶ Comptroller General of the U.S.

- ▸ Secretary of Education
- ▸ U.S. Attorney General (for law enforcement purposes only)
- ▸ State and local educational authorities
- ◆ School officials determined by the institution to have a legitimate educational interest
- ◆ Agents acting on behalf of the institution (*e.g.* contractors, consultants)
- ◆ Schools in which the student seeks or intends to enroll (additional conditions exist)
- ◆ A party, such as the Department of Veteran's Affairs or an employer, providing financial aid to the student ("financial aid" does not include any payments made by parents); (additional conditions exist)
- ◆ Organizations conducting studies for or on behalf of educational institutions (additional conditions exist)
- ◆ Accrediting organizations for accreditation purposes
- ◆ Parents of a dependent student (as defined by the IRS code)
- ◆ Parents when their student (under 21) is found to have violated the alcohol or drug policy of the institution
- ◆ To comply with a judicial order or subpoena, including *ex parte* orders under the USA Patriot Act
- ◆ Appropriate parties if a health or safety emergency exists and the information will assist in resolving the emergency (additional conditions exist)
- ◆ The student
- ◆ An alleged victim of a crime of violence when the disclosure is the results of a disciplinary hearing regarding the alleged perpetrator of that crime with respect to that crime
- ◆ Anyone requesting the final results of a disciplinary hearing against an alleged perpetrator who has been found in violation of the campus code relating to a crime of violence or non-forcible sex offense
- ◆ The Department of Homeland Security (DHS), Immigration and Customs Enforcement (ICE) for purpose of complying with Request Form ICE relative to the institution's participation in SEVIS
- ◆ Military recruiters who request "Student Recruiting Information" for recruiting purposes only (Solomon Amendment). Student recruiting information is name, address, telephone listing, age (or year of birth), class

level, major, degrees received and most recent educational institution of enrollment. (conditions exist)

- The Internal Revenue Service (IRS), for purposes of complying with the *Taxpayer Relief Act of 1997*
- Anyone, when the disclosure concerns information provided by sex offenders required to register under state or federal law

How does technology impact FERPA guidelines?

As we move toward an environment with less paper, it is important to note that the same principles of access and confidentiality must be applied to all media, including but not limited to, electronic data, email, and video or audio tapes.

What happens if a college does *not* comply with FERPA?

The Department of Education may issue a notice to cease the non-compliance and could ultimately withhold funds administered by the Secretary of Education.

Where can I get more information regarding FERPA?

Family Policy Compliance Office
U.S. Department of Education
400 Maryland Avenue, SW
Washington, DC 20202–5901
Phone (202) 260–3887
Fax (202) 260–9001
Email: ferpa@ed.gov
Web: www.ed.gov/policy/gen/guid/fpco/index.html

Assistance is also available from AACRAO at ferpa@aacrao.org.

◇◇◇◇◇◇◇◇◇◇◇◇◇◇◇◇◇◇◇◇◇

CHAPTER THREE

Definition of Terms

Understanding key terms is essential to the interpretation of The Act and the final regulations for its implementation. Some definitions and explanations which carry substantive meaning for understanding The Act are listed here for the convenience of the reader. The regulations, as contained in Appendix A to this guide, provide all legal definitions.

ACT: Refers to the *Family Educational Rights and Privacy Act of 1974*, as amended, enacted as Section 444 of the *General Education Provisions Act* (20 U.S.C. 1232g).

AGENCY: An organization, company, or bureau that provides some service for another; a company having a franchise to represent another.

AGENT: A person or business formally authorized to act on another's behalf, *e.g.* within the scope of a contract between the two parties.

ALLEGED PERPETRATOR OF A CRIME OF VIOLENCE: A student who is alleged to have committed a crime of violence or a non-forcible sex offense.

ALUMNI RECORD: A record created by an educational institution that may contain personally identifiable information about a former student; is related solely to that student's activities as an alumnus; and is not related to attendance as a student.

ALUMNUS: A graduate or former student of a specific school, college, or university

ATTENDANCE: Includes but is not limited to:

◆ Attendance in person or by paper correspondence, videoconference, satellite, Internet, or other electronic information and telecommunications technologies for students who are not physically present in the classroom; and

◆ The period during which a person is working in a work-study program.

BIOMETRIC RECORD: As used in the definition of "personally identifiable information," a record of one or more measurable biological or behavioral characteristics that can be used for automated recognition of an individual. Examples include fingerprints; retina and iris patterns; voiceprints; DNA sequence; facial characteristics; and handwriting.

C.F.R.: See "Code of Federal Regulations."

CLERY ACT: The *Jeanne Clery Disclosure of Campus Security Policy and Campus Crime Statistics Act,* codified at 20 U.S.C. 1092 (f) as a part of the *Higher Education Act of 1965*, is a federal law that requires colleges and universities to disclose certain timely and annual information about campus crime and security policies. All public and private postsecondary educational institutions participating in federal student aid programs are subject to it. The Clery Act was originally enacted by Congress in 1990 as the Campus Security Act. It requires colleges and universities to publish an annual report every year by October 1st containing three years worth of crime statistics and certain security policy statements, including sexual assault policies, which assure basic victims' rights, the law enforcement authority of campus police and where the students should go to report crimes.

CODE OF FEDERAL REGULATIONS: The annual accumulation of executive agency regulations published in the daily Federal Register, combined with regulations issued previously and still in effect. The C.F.R. contains the general body of regulatory laws governing practice and procedure before federal administrative agencies. The regulations pertaining to FERPA are found in 34 C.F.R. Part 99 (*see* Appendix A, on page 37).

CONTRACTOR: Outside parties who, for the purposes of The Act, qualify as school officials in that they are acting for the agency or institution and are subject to the same conditions governing the access and use of records that apply to other school officials.

COURT ORDER: A directive issued by a Court of Law, requiring an entity to take some specified action.

CRIME OF VIOLENCE: Refers to acts that would, if proven, constitute any of the following offenses or attempts to commit the following offenses: arson, assault offenses, burglary, negligent homicide, criminal homicide, destruction/damage/vandalism of property, kidnapping/abduction, robbery, forcible sex offenses.

DATES OF ATTENDANCE: The period of time during which a student attends or attended an institution. Examples of dates of attendance include an academic year, a spring semester, or a first quarter. The term does not include specific daily records or a student's attendance at the institution.

DE-IDENTIFIED RECORDS AND INFORMATION: An educational record that has had all personally identifiable information, as defined in §99.31(b), removed.

DIGITAL MILLENNIUM COPYRIGHT ACT, THE: The Recording Industry Association of America continues to issue hundreds of subpoenas for names and addresses of students whose internet service provider address or internet names correlate to evidence of music sharing. In response to campus inquiries about whether or not to disclose an education record pursuant to a subpoena, the FPCO advises that institutions may do so *as long as* a reasonable attempt is made to give the student prior notice.

DIRECTORY INFORMATION: Information contained in an education record of a student that would not generally be considered harmful or an invasion of privacy if disclosed. It includes, but is not limited to, the student's name; address; telephone listing; electronic mail address; photograph; date and place of birth; major field of study; grade level; enrollment status (*e.g.*, undergraduate or graduate, full-time or part-time); dates of attendance; participation in officially recognized activities and sports; weight and height of members of athletic teams; degrees, honors and awards received; and the most recent educational agency or institution attended.

(a) Directory information does *not* include a student's—(1) Social security number; or (2) Student identification (ID) number, except as provided in paragraph (b) of this section.

(b) Directory information includes a student ID number, user ID, or other unique personal identifier used by the student for purposes of accessing or communicating in electronic systems, but only if the identifier cannot be used to gain access to education records except when used in conjunction with one or more factors that authenticate the user's identity, such as a personal identification number (PIN), password, or other factor known or possessed only by the authorized user.

NON-DISCLOSURE / OPT OUT / NO RELEASE OF DIRECTORY INFORMATION: The requirement that an educational institution must provide the opportunity for a student to refuse to let the institution release information designated as Directory Information, as outlined in §99.37.

DISCIPLINARY ACTION OR PROCEEDING: The investigation, adjudication, or imposition of sanctions by an educational agency or institution with respect to an infraction or violation of the internal rules of conduct applicable to students of the agency or institution.

"FINAL RESULTS" OF A DISCIPLINARY PROCEEDING: A decision or determination, made by an honor court or council, committee, commission, or other entity authorized to resolve disciplinary matters within the institution. The disclosure of final results must include only the name of the student, the violation committed, and any sanction imposed by the institution against the student.

DISCLOSURE: To permit access to, or the release, transfer, or other communication of, personally identifiable information contained in education records by any means, including oral, written, or electronic means, to any party except the party identified as the party that provided or created the record.

EASILY TRACEABLE: This term was removed from the new regulations and replaced with the language in §99.3, "personally identifiable information," (f) and (g).

ELECTRONIC SIGNATURE: An electronic sound, symbol, or process, attached to or logically associated with a contract or other record and executed or adopted by a person with the intent to sign the record that identifies and authenticates that person as the source of the electronic consent, and indicates such person's approval of the information contained in the electronic consent.

EDI: *See* "Electronic Data Interchange," on page 18.

EDUCATIONAL INSTITUTION (OR AGENCY): Generally means any public or private agency, institution (including governing boards which provide administrative control or direction of a university system) of postsecondary education, which receives funds from any federal program under the administrative responsibility of the Secretary of Education. The term refers to the institution as a whole, including all of its components (*e.g.*, schools or departments in a university).

EDUCATION RECORDS: Those records directly related to a student and maintained by the institution or by a party acting for the institution.

The term "education records" does not include the following:

(1) Records that are kept in the sole possession of the maker, are used only as a personal memory aid, and are not accessible or revealed to any other person except a temporary substitute for the maker of the record.

(2) Records of the law enforcement unit of an educational agency or institution, subject to the provisions of § 99.8.

(3)(i) Records relating to an individual who is employed by an educational agency or institution, that:

(A) Are made and maintained in the normal course of business;

(B) Relate exclusively to the individual in that individual's capacity as an employee; and

(C) Are not available for use for any other purpose.

(ii) Records relating to an individual in attendance at the agency or institution who is employed as a result of his or her status as a student are education records and not excepted under paragraph (3)(i) of this definition.

(4) Records on a student who is 18 years of age or older, or is attending an institution of postsecondary education, that are:

(i) Made or maintained by a physician, psychiatrist, psychologist, or other recognized professional or paraprofessional acting in his or her professional capacity or assisting in a paraprofessional capacity;

(ii) Made, maintained, or used only in connection with treatment of the student; and

(iii) Disclosed only to individuals providing the treatment. For the purpose of this definition, "treatment" does not include remedial educational activities or activities that are part of the program of instruction at the agency or institution;

(5) Records created or received by an educational agency or institution after an individual is no longer a student in attendance and that are not directly related to the individual's attendance as a student.

(6) Grades on peer-graded papers before they are collected and recorded by a teacher.

ELECTRONIC DATA INTERCHANGE: Utilizes standard data formats for transmitting data from one computer to another.

ELIGIBLE STUDENT: Refers to a student who has reached the age of 18 *or* is attending an institution of postsecondary education. Since these guidelines are specifically for postsecondary institutions, "student" as used in this document is presumed always to refer to an eligible student. In non-postsecondary institutions, parents of students have additional rights not covered in this guide.

ENROLLED STUDENT: For the purposes of this publication, this term refers to a student who has satisfied all of the institutional requirements for attendance at the institution. The Family Policy Compliance Office has stated that each institution may determine when a student is *"in attendance"* in accordance with its own enrollment procedures. (*Federal Register*, July 6, 2000, p. 41856).

EX PARTE ORDER: An order issued by a court of competent jurisdiction without notice to an adverse party in connection with the investigation or prosecution of terrorism crimes specified in sections 2331 and 2332b(g)(5)(B) of Title 18, U.S. Code.

FAMILY POLICY COMPLIANCE OFFICE: The office within the U.S. Department of Education that is responsible for enforcing/administering the *Family Educational Rights and Privacy Act of 1974* as amended. This office has responsibility for FERPA at all levels of education (K–12, postsecondary).

FINANCIAL AID: A payment of funds to an individual (or a payment in kind of tangible or intangible property to the individual), which is conditioned on the individual's attendance at an educational agency or institution. Financial aid does not include payments made by parents.

GRAMM-LEACH-BLILEY: The *Gramm-Leach-Bliley Act of 1999* prohibits an institution that provides financial products or services from sharing a customer's "nonpublic personal information" with non-affiliated third parties unless the institution first discloses its privacy policy to consumers and allows them to "opt out" of that disclosure. The Act restricts the ability to sell, give or otherwise disclose personal information to third parties without permission.

HEALTH AND SAFETY EMERGENCY: An educational agency or institution may disclose personally identifiable information from an educational record to appropriate parties including parents of an eligible student, in connection with an emergency if knowledge of the information is necessary to protect the health or safety of the student or other individuals.

HIPAA: The *Health Insurance Portability and Accountability Act of 1996* requires the establishment of national standards for electronic health care transactions and national identifiers for providers, health insurance plans, and employers with the intention of keeping patient information private.

"IN ATTENDANCE" (OR WHEN IS A STUDENT "IN ATTENDANCE"?)**:** *See* "Enrolled Student" on page 18.

INSTITUTION OF POSTSECONDARY EDUCATION: An institution that provides education to students beyond the secondary school level. "Secondary school level" means the educational level (not beyond grade 12) at which secondary education is provided.

LAW ENFORCEMENT UNIT: Any individual or other component of an institution, including commissioned police officers and noncommissioned security guards, officially authorized by the institution to enforce any local, state, or federal law and maintain the physical security and safety of the institution. (Although the unit may perform other non-law enforcement functions, it retains its status as a law enforcement unit.)

LAW ENFORCEMENT UNIT RECORDS: These records are not education records as defined by The Act, so long as the records are files, documents, and other materials that are: 1) created by a law enforcement unit, 2) created for a law enforcement purpose, and 3) maintained by the law enforcement unit. Law enforcement records *do not* include: 1) records created by a law enforcement unit for law enforcement purposes other than those of the law enforcement unit; 2) records created and maintained by a law enforcement unit exclusively for non–law enforcement purposes, such as a disciplinary action or proceeding conducted by the institution.

LEGITIMATE EDUCATIONAL INTEREST: The demonstrated "need to know" by those officials of an institution who act in the student's educational interest, including faculty, administration, clerical and professional employees, and other persons who manage student record information including student employees or agents. (Although The Act does not define "legitimate educational interest," it states that institutions must establish their own criteria, according to their own procedures and requirements, for determining when their school officials have a legitimate educational interest in a student's education records.) *See* the "FERPA Model Notification of Rights" in Appendix C, on page 81, which contains sample language.

MEGAN'S LAW: Established the minimum national standards for sex offender registration and community notification programs. States must establish programs that require a sexually violent predator (and anyone convicted of specified criminal offenses against minors) to register their name and address with the appropriate authority where the offender lives, works, or is enrolled as a student. States are also required to release relevant information necessary to protect the public concerning persons required to register, excluding the identity of any victim. Under FERPA, prior consent is not required if the disclosure concerns sex offenders under Section 170101 of the *Violent Crime Control and Law Enforcement Act of 1994*, 42 U.S.C. 14071, and the information was provided to the educational agency or institution under 42 U.S.C. 14071 and applicable federal guidelines.

NON-DISCLOSURE / OPT OUT / NO RELEASE OF DIRECTORY INFORMATION: *See* "Directory Information" on page 15.

NON-FORCIBLE SEX OFFENSE: Statutory rape or incest.

OUTSOURCING: The circumstances under which a business contracts with another business to conduct a service or function that it would otherwise provide itself. In many cases the contracted business will be acting as an "agent" (*see also* "Agent" on page 13) of the contracting business.

PARENT: Includes a natural parent (custodial and/or non-custodial), a guardian, or an individual acting as a parent in the absence of a parent or a guardian.

PARTY: Refers to an individual, agency, institution, or organization.

PERSONALLY IDENTIFIABLE: Data or information which includes, but is not limited to—(a) The student's name; (b) The name of the student's parent or other family members; (c) The address of the student or student's family;

(d) A personal identifier, such as the student's social security number, student number, or biometric record; (e) Other indirect identifiers, such as the student's date of birth, place of birth, and mother's maiden name; (f) Other information that, alone or in combination, is linked or linkable to a specific student that would allow a reasonable person in the school community, who does not have personal knowledge of the relevant circumstances, to identify the student with reasonable certainty; or (g) Information requested by a person who the educational agency or institution reasonably believes knows the identity of the student to whom the education record relates.

RECORD: Any information or data recorded in any medium (*e.g.*, handwriting, print, tapes, film, microfilm, microfiche, any form of electronic data storage including emails).

RECORDKEEPING: Recordation of releases of personally identifiable information from a student's education records to a party outside of the institution. Includes health or safety emergency releases. *See* §99.32 of the FERPA regulations (on page 61) for more details, including exceptions.

REDISCLOSURE: Notification requirement for institutions of higher education and state educational authorities acting on behalf of the institution, concerning the disclosure of personally identifiable information from education records to parties outside the institution. See §99.33 (on page 64) for details, including exceptions.

REGULATIONS, THE: Federal regulations implementing the statutory requirements of FERPA and found in Appendix A (on page 37). Also cited in this publication as 34 C.F.R. Part 99. Throughout this Guide, we have eliminated the "C.F.R." symbol where possible and have substituted the section symbol (§) before the specific regulation discussed.

SEVIS: The Student and Exchange Visitor Information System (SEVIS) is an Internet-based system that establishes a process for electronic reporting by designated school officials of information required to be reported to the Department of Homeland Security's Immigration and Customs Enforcement (ICE), previously known as the Immigration and Naturalization Service (INS). SEVIS maintains accurate and current information on non-immigrant students (F and M visa), exchange visitors (J visa), and their dependents (F-2, M-2, and J-2). SEVIS enables schools and program sponsors to transmit mandatory information and event notifications via the Internet, to the Department of Homeland Security, Immigration and Customs Enforcement (ICE) throughout a student's or exchange visitor's stay in the United States, in order to certify an institution as eligible to participate in SEVIS.

SCHOOL OFFICIALS: Those members of an institution who act in the student's educational interest within the limitations of their "need to know." These may include faculty, administration, clerical and professional employees and other persons who manage student education record information including student employees or agents. It may also include contractors, volunteers, and others performing institutional functions. (Although The Act does not define "school officials," it states that institutions must establish their own criteria, according to their own procedures and requirements for determining them. This is a recommended definition.)

SOLE POSSESSION RECORDS: Records that are kept in the sole possession of the maker, are used only as a personal memory aid, and are not accessible or revealed to any other person except a temporary substitute for the maker of the record. Any record that is made in conjunction with a student or other school official, such as an evaluation of a student or the student's performance, is *not* a sole possession record.

SOLOMON AMENDMENT: Sometimes referred to in this publication simply as "Solomon." This 1996 amendment requires postsecondary institutions to provide Department of Defense representatives, among other things, access to student recruiting information (defined below).

STUDENT: Any individual for whom an educational institution maintains education records. The term does not include an individual who has not been in attendance at the institution. An individual who is or has been enrolled in one component unit of an institution and applies for admission to a second unit has no right to inspect the records accumulated by the second unit until enrolled therein.

STUDENT RECRUITING INFORMATION: Information identified in the Solomon Amendment that institutions are required to provide military recruiters upon request. Those items are: student name, addresses, telephone listings, age or year of birth, class level, academic major, degrees received and the most recent previous educational institution in which the student was enrolled.

STUDENT RIGHT-TO-KNOW ACT OF 1990: Referred to in this publication as SRTK. SRTK requires colleges and universities to report graduation rates to current and prospective students.

SUBPOENA: A command from a court to require the person named in the subpoena to appear at a stated time and place to provide testimony or evidence. There are two main types of subpoenas: *duces tecum* (requires the production of documents, papers or other tangibles) and *ad testificandum* (requires person to testify in a particular court case).

USA PATRIOT ACT: The *Uniting and Strengthening America by Providing Appropriate Tools Required to Intercept and Obstruct Terrorism (USA PATRIOT) Act of 2001* permits a postsecondary institution to disclose personally identifiable information from a student's education records—without notification of the student—to the U.S. Attorney General or his designee in order to comply with an *ex parte* order in connection with the investigation or prosecution of an offense listed in 18 U.S.C. 2332(g)(5)(B).

U.S.C.: United States Code. A compilation of all federal legislation organized into 50 titles. Revised every six years with supplementary volumes issued in intervening years. The legislation related to FERPA is found in 20 U.S.C. 1232g.

CHAPTER FOUR

FERPA Basics for Faculty and Instructors

The following document is intended to serve as a summary of FERPA, particularly focused toward faculty and instructional staff. It can be used as a handout as well as a training tool.

The Essence of FERPA

◆ Federal law designed to protect the privacy of education records. It also provides guidelines for appropriately using and releasing student education records.

◆ It is intended that students' rights be broadly defined and applied. Therefore, consider the student as the "*owner*" of the information in his or her education record, and the institution as the "*custodian*" of that record.

Key Terms/Definitions

"EDUCATION RECORDS" include any record maintained by the institution that contains information that is personally identifiable to a student (in whatever format or medium) with some narrowly defined exceptions:

◆ Records in the "sole possession of the maker" (*e.g.*, private advising notes).

◆ Law enforcement records created and maintained by a law enforcement agency for a law enforcement purpose.

◆ Employment records (unless the employment is based on student status). The employment records of student employees (*e.g.*, work-study, wages, graduate teaching associates) are part of their education records.

◆ Medical/psychological treatment records (*e.g.*, from a health or counseling center).

◆ Alumni records (*i.e.*, those created after the student graduated or left the institution).

"DIRECTORY INFORMATION:" Those data items that are generally not considered harmful or an invasion of privacy if publicly available. This information cannot be released if student has a "no release" on his or her record. Each institution establishes what it considers to be directory information. Common examples include: name, address (local, home and email), telephone (local and home), academic program of study, dates of attendance, date of birth, most recent educational institution attended, and degrees and awards received.

◆ Directory information *cannot* include: race, gender, SSN (or part of an SSN), grades, GPA, country of citizenship, or religion. Except in very specific circumstances, a student ID number (SIN) also cannot be considered directory information.

◆ Every student must be given the opportunity to have directory information suppressed from public release. This process is often referred to as a "no release," "opt out" or "suppression." When a student makes this request, everyone within the institution must abide by a student's request that no information be released about the student.

◆ It is important to understand, that a "no release" does *not* mean that a school official within the institution who has a demonstrated legitimate educational interest (*e.g.*, a faculty member teaching the student in class) is precluded from using the information to perform that official's job duties.

"PARENT:" With reference to FERPA, the term "parent" refers to either parent (including custodial and non-custodial, if divorced).

When do FERPA rights begin?

A FERPA-related college education record begins for a student when he or she enrolls in a higher education institution. At a postsecondary institution, rights belong to the student in attendance, regardless of the student's age.

Basic Rights of Students under the Act

◆ Be notified of their FERPA rights at least annually.
◆ Inspect and review their records.
◆ Amend an incorrect record.
◆ Consent to disclosure (with exceptions).

ANNUAL NOTIFICATION

Every institution must notify students of their FERPA rights at least annually.

INSPECTION AND REVIEW

Students have the *right* to see everything in their "education record," except:
◆ Information about other students;
◆ Financial records of parents; and
◆ Confidential letters of recommendation if they waived their right of access.

FERPA does not prescribe what records are created or how long they are to be kept; however, you cannot destroy a record if there is a request to inspect and review. It is important to know and understand your institution's records retention policy.

RIGHT TO CONSENT TO DISCLOSURE

Start with the premise that the student has the right to control to whom his or her education record is released. Then, there are several exceptions when that permission is not required.

In those instances where a signed release is required, regulations now provide the flexibility to accept an electronic signature.

When is prior consent not required?

The institution may disclose records without consent if certain requirements are met, but it is not required to do so.

Some examples of the exceptions to the release requirement include:

◆ "School officials" with a "legitimate educational interest." Employees and legal agents have access to education records in order to perform their official, educationally-related duties.

◆ Disclosure to organizations conducting studies to improve instruction, or to accrediting organizations.

◆ Disclosure to parents of *dependent students* (IRS definition); Check to see how your institution expects parents to demonstrate student dependent status.

◆ To comply with a judicial order or lawfully issued subpoena.

◆ Disclosure for a health/safety emergency (must document what the emergency was and to whom the information was released).

◆ Disclosure of directory information, provided the student has not requested "no release."

Some Specific Issues for Faculty and Instructional Staff

◆ **POSTING GRADES:** Since grades can never be directory information, it is inappropriate to post grades in a public setting. An instructor may, however, post grades if the grades are posted in such a manner that only the instructor and the individual student can identify the individual and his or her grade. Grades should never be posted by any portion of the SSN. Additionally, it is recommended that such a posted list should not be in the same order as the class roster or in alphabetical order.

◆ **WEB-BASED TOOLS TO SUPPORT CLASSES:** Courses supported by class Web sites and/or discussion groups must take extra precautions to not inadvertently release non-directory student information. Only directory information can be available to the general public and other class members, so it is recommended that such Web-based tools employ a security layer so that only class members and instructors can access appropriate information.

◆ **STUDENTS OPTING FOR NO RELEASE IN THE CLASSROOM SETTING:** Students cannot choose to be anonymous in the classroom setting. If a student has chosen "no release" for his or her directory information, that does not mean that an instructor cannot call on him or her by name in class or that the student's email address cannot be displayed on an electronic classroom support tool such as a discussion board, blog, or chat feature.

CHAPTER FIVE

◇◇◇◇◇◇◇◇◇◇◇◇◇◇◇◇◇

FERPA Basics for Administrative Staff

The following document is intended to serve as a summary of FERPA, particularly focused toward staff in an office that regularly works with student education records. It can be used as a handout as well as a training tool.

The Essence of FERPA

◆ Federal law designed to protect the privacy of education records. It also provides guidelines for appropriately using and releasing student education records.

◆ It is intended that students' rights be broadly defined and applied. Therefore, consider the student as the "*owner*" of the information in his or her education record, and the institution as the "*custodian*" of that record.

Key Terms/Definitions

"EDUCATION RECORDS" include any record maintained by the institution that contains information that is personally identifiable to a student (in whatever format or medium) with some narrowly defined exceptions:

◆ Records in the "sole possession of the maker" (*e.g.*. private advising notes).

◆ Law enforcement records created and maintained by a law enforcement agency for a law enforcement purpose.

- Employment records (unless the employment is based on student status). The employment records of student employees (*e.g.*, work-study, wages, graduate teaching associates) are part of their education records.
- Medical/psychological treatment records (*e.g.*, from a health or counseling center).
- Alumni records (*i.e.*, those created after the student graduated or left the institution).

"DIRECTORY INFORMATION:" Those data items that are generally not considered harmful or an invasion of privacy if publicly available. Cannot be released if student has a "no release" on his or her record. Each institution establishes what it considers to be directory information. Common examples include: name, address (local, home and email), telephone (local and home), academic program of study, dates of attendance, date of birth, most recent educational institution attended, and degrees and awards received.

- Directory information *cannot* include: race, gender, SSN (or part of an SSN), grades, GPA, country of citizenship, or religion. Except in very specific circumstances, a student ID number (SIN) also cannot be considered directory information.
- Every student must be given the opportunity to have directory information suppressed from public release. This process is often referred to as a "no release," "opt out" or "suppression." Everyone within the institution must abide by a student's request that no information be released about the student.
- It is important to understand, that a "no release" does *not* mean that a school official within the institution who has a demonstrated legitimate educational interest (*e.g.*, faculty member teaching the student in class) is precluded from using the information to perform that official's job duties.

"PARENT:" With reference to FERPA, the term "parent" refers to either parent (including custodial and non-custodial, if divorced).

When do FERPA rights begin?

A FERPA-related college education record begins for a student when he or she enrolls in a higher education institution. At a postsecondary institution, rights belong to the student in attendance, regardless of the student's age.

Basic Rights of Students under the Act:

◆ Be notified of their FERPA rights at least annually.
◆ Inspect and review their records.
◆ Amend an incorrect record.
◆ Consent to disclosure (with exceptions).

ANNUAL NOTIFICATION

Every institution must notify students of their FERPA rights at least annually.

INSPECTION AND REVIEW

Students have the *right* to see everything in their "education record," except:
◆ Information about other students.
◆ Financial records of parents.
◆ Confidential letters of recommendation if they waived their right of access.

FERPA does not prescribe what records are created or how long they are to be kept; however, you cannot destroy a record once there is a request to inspect and review. It is important to know and understand your institution's records retention policy.

RIGHT TO CONSENT TO DISCLOSURE

Start with the premise that the student has the right to control to whom his or her education record is released. Then, there are several exceptions when that permission is not required.

In those instances where a signed release is required, regulations now provide the flexibility to accept an electronic signature.

When is prior consent not required?

The institution may disclose records without consent if certain requirements are met, but it is not required to do so. Some examples of the exceptions to the release requirement include:

- ◆ "School officials" with a "legitimate educational interest." Employees and legal agents have access to education records in order to perform their official, educationally-related duties.
- ◆ Disclosure to another institution where the student seeks to enroll or is enrolled.
- ◆ Disclosure to DOE, state/local education authorities.
- ◆ Disclosure in connection with the receipt of financial aid.
- ◆ Disclosure to state/local officials in conjunction with legislative requirements.
- ◆ Disclosure to organizations conducting studies to improve instruction, or to accrediting organizations.
- ◆ Disclosure to parents of *dependent students* (IRS definition). Check to see how your institution expects parents to demonstrate student dependent status.
- ◆ To comply with a judicial order or lawfully issued subpoena.
- ◆ Disclosure for a health/safety emergency (must document what the emergency was and to whom the information was released).
- ◆ Disclosure of directory information provided the student has not requested "no release."
- ◆ Disciplinary information:
  - ► Disclosure to the alleged victim of a crime of violence, such as information from disciplinary proceedings.
  - ► *Only* when found in violation, and *only* for crimes of violence — release of name, sanction and outcome can be made to anyone.
- ◆ Disclosure to parents of any student under the age of 21, a violation of federal, state, local or institutional laws/regulations related to substance abuse (provided that other laws governing the institution, such as state law, do not preclude such disclosures).

FERPA rights at a postsecondary institution end with a student's death. However, state law may provide for a continued right to privacy in your state. Students have a formal right to file a complaint with the Department of Education.

Key Resources for Additional Information:

◆ Your campus registrar
◆ AACRAO (Compliance)—www.aacrao.org/compliance/ferpa/
◆ Family Compliance Office of the Department of Education (administers FERPA compliance)— www.ed.gov/policy/gen/guid/fpco/

∞∞∞∞∞∞∞∞∞∞∞∞∞

Family Educational Rights and Privacy Act Regulations

Note: To access a copy of the Family Educational Rights and Privacy Act of 1974 as Amended go to http://codes.lp.findlaw.com/uscode/20/31/III/4/1232g.

(Amendments made in 2009 have been highlighted for the convenience of readers.)

34 CFR Part 99

Subpart A—General

Section

99.1 To which educational agencies or institutions do these regulations apply?

99.2 What is the purpose of these regulations?

99.3 What definitions apply to these regulations?

99.4 What are the rights of parents?

99.5 What are the rights of students?

99.7 What must an educational agency or institution include in its annual notification?

99.8 What provisions apply to records of a law enforcement unit?

Subpart B—What Are the Rights of Inspection and Review of Education Records?

Section

99.10 What rights exist for a parent or eligible student to inspect and review education records?

99.11 May an educational agency or institution charge a fee for copies of education records?

99.12 What limitations exist on the right to inspect and review records?

Subpart C—What Are the Procedures for Amending Educating Records?

Section

99.20 How can a parent or eligible student request amendment of the student's education records?

99.21 Under what conditions does a parent or eligible student have the right to a hearing?

99.22 What minimum requirements exist for the conduct of a hearing?

Subpart D—May an Educational Agency or Institution Disclose Personally Identifiable Information from Education Records?

Section

99.30 Under what conditions is prior consent required to disclose information?

99.31 Under what conditions is prior consent not required to disclose information?

99.32 What recordkeeping requirements exist concerning requests and disclosures?

99.33 What limitations apply to the redisclosure of information?

99.34 What conditions apply to disclosure of information to other educational agencies or institutions?

99.35 What conditions apply to disclosure of information for federal or state program purposes?

99.36 What conditions apply to disclosure of information in health and safety emergencies?

Subpart A—General

§ 99.1 TO WHICH EDUCATIONAL AGENCIES OR INSTITUTIONS DO THESE REGULATIONS APPLY?

(a) Except as otherwise noted in § 99.10, this part applies to an educational
agency or institution to which funds have been made available under any
program administered by the Secretary, if—

   (1) The education institution provides educational services or instruction, or both, to students; or

   (2) The educational agency is authorized to direct and control public elementary or secondary, or postsecondary educational institutions.

(b) This part does not apply to an educational agency or institution solely because students attending that agency or institution receive non-monetary benefits under a program referenced in paragraph (a) of this section, if no funds under that program are made available to the agency or institution.

(c) The Secretary considers funds to be made available to an educational agency or institution if funds under one or more of the programs referenced in paragraph (a) of this section—

(1) Are provided to the agency or institution by grant, cooperative agreement, contract, subgrant, or subcontract; or

(2) Are provided to students attending the agency or institution and the funds may be paid to the agency or institution by those students for educational purposes, such as under the Pell Grant Program and the Guaranteed Student Loan Program (Titles IV-A-1 and IV-B, respectively, of the *Higher Education Act of 1965*, as amended).

(d) If an educational agency or institution receives funds under one or more of the programs covered by this section, the regulations in this part apply to the recipient as a whole, including each of its components (such as a department within a university).

[Authority: 20 u.s.c. 1232g]

§ 99.2 WHAT IS THE PURPOSE OF THESE REGULATIONS?

The purpose of this part is to set out requirements for the protection of privacy of parents and students under section 444 of the *General Education Provisions Act*, as amended.

[Authority: 20 u.s.c. 1232g]

§ 99.3 WHAT DEFINITIONS APPLY TO THESE REGULATIONS?

The following definitions apply to this part:

"ACT" means the *Family Educational Rights and Privacy Act of 1974*, as amended, enacted as section 444 of the *General Education Provisions Act*.

[Authority: 20 u.s.c. 1232g]

"ATTENDANCE" includes, but is not limited to:

(a) Attendance in person or by paper correspondence, videoconference, satellite, Internet, or other electronic information and telecommunications technologies for students who are not physically present in the classroom; and

(b) The period during which a person is working under a work-study program.

[Authority: 20 U.S.C. 1232g]

"BIOMETRIC RECORD," as used in the definition of "personally identifiable information," means a record of one or more measurable biological or behavioral characteristics that can be used for automated recognition of an individual. Examples include fingerprints; retina and iris patterns; voiceprints; DNA sequence; facial characteristics; and handwriting.

[Authority: 20 U.S.C. 1232g]

"DATES OF ATTENDANCE." (a) The term means the period of time during which a student attends or attended an educational agency or institution. Examples of dates of attendance include an academic year, a spring semester, or a first quarter.

(b) The term does not include specific daily records of a student's attendance at an educational agency or institution.

[Authority: 20 U.S.C. 1232g(a)(5)(A)]

"DIRECTORY INFORMATION" means information contained in an education record of a student that would not generally be considered harmful or an invasion of privacy if disclosed.

(a) Directory information includes, but is not limited to, the student's name, address, telephone listing, electronic mail address, photograph, date and place of birth, major field of study, dates of attendance, grade level, enrollment status (*e.g.*, undergraduate or graduate; full-time or part-time), participation in officially recognized activities and sports, weight and height of members of athletic teams, degrees, honors and awards received, and the most recent educational agency or institution attended.

(b) Directory information does not include a student's:

(1) Social security number; or

(2) Student identification (ID) number, except as provided in paragraph (c) of this section.

(c) Directory information includes a student ID number, user ID, or other unique personal identifier used by the student for purposes of accessing or communicating in electronic systems, but only if the identifier cannot be used to gain access to education records except when used in conjunction with one or more factors that authenticate the user's identity, such as a personal identification number (PIN), password, or other factor known or possessed only by the authorized user.

[Authority: 20 U.S.C. 1232g(a)(5)(A)]

"DISCIPLINARY ACTION OR PROCEEDING" means the investigation, adjudication, or imposition of sanctions by an educational agency or institution with respect to an infraction or violation of the internal rules of conduct applicable to students of the agency or institution.

"DISCLOSURE" means to permit access to or the release, transfer, or other communication of personally identifiable information contained in education records to any party, by any means, including oral, written, or electronic means. Disclosure means to permit access to or the release, transfer, or other communication of personally identifiable information contained in education records by any m eans, including oral, written, or electronic means, to any party except the party identified as the party that provided or created the record.

[Authority: 20 U.S.C. 1232g(b)(1) and (b)(2)]

"EDUCATIONAL AGENCY OR INSTITUTION" means any public or private agency or institution to which this part applies under § 99.1(a).

[Authority: 20 U.S.C. 1232g(a)(3)]

"EDUCATION RECORDS" (a) The term means those records that are:

(1) Directly related to a student; and

(2) Maintained by an educational agency or institution or by a party acting for the agency or institution.

(b) The term does not include:

(1) Records that are kept in the sole possession of the maker, are used only as a personal memory aid, and are not accessible or revealed to any other person except a temporary substitute for the maker of the record.

(2) Records of the law enforcement unit of an educational agency or institution, subject to the provisions of § 99.8.

(3)(i) Records relating to an individual who is employed by an educational agency or institution, that:

(A) Are made and maintained in the normal course of business;
(B) Relate exclusively to the individual in that individual's capacity as an employee; and
(C) Are not available for use for any other purpose.

(ii) Records relating to an individual in attendance at the agency or institution who is employed as a result of his or her status as a student are education records and not excepted under paragraph (b) (3)(i) of this definition.

(4) Records on a student who is 18 years of age or older, or is attending an institution of postsecondary education, that are:

(i) Made or maintained by a physician, psychiatrist, psychologist, or other recognized professional or paraprofessional acting in his or her professional capacity or assisting in a paraprofessional capacity;
(ii) Made, maintained, or used only in connection with treatment of the student; and
(iii) Disclosed only to individuals providing the treatment. For the purpose of this definition, "treatment" does not include remedial educational activities or activities that are part of the program of instruction at the agency or institution; and

(5) Records created or received by an educational agency or institution after an individual is no longer a student in attendance and that are not directly related to the individual's attendance as a student.

(6) Grades on peer-graded papers before they are collected and recorded by a teacher.

[Authority: 20 u.s.c. 1232g(a)(4)]

"ELIGIBLE STUDENT" means a student who has reached 18 years of age or is attending an institution of postsecondary education.

[Authority: 20 u.s.c. 1232g(d)]

"INSTITUTION OF POSTSECONDARY EDUCATION" means an institution that provides education to students beyond the secondary school level; "secondary school level" means the educational level (not beyond grade 12) at which secondary education is provided as determined under state law.

[Authority: 20 u.s.c. 1232g(d)]

"PARENT" means a parent of a student and includes a natural parent, a guardian, or an individual acting as a parent in the absence of a parent or a guardian.

[Authority: 20 u.s.c. 1232g]

"PARTY" means an individual, agency, institution, or organization.

[Authority: 20 u.s.c. 1232g(b)(4)(A)]

"PERSONALLY IDENTIFIABLE INFORMATION" includes, but is not limited to:

(a) The student's name;
(b) The name of the student's parent or other family members;
(c) The address of the student or student's family;
(d) A personal identifier, such as the student's social security number or student number, or biometric record;
(e) Other indirect identifiers, such as the student's date of birth, place of birth, and mother's maiden name;
(f) Other information that, alone or in combination, is linked or linkable to a specific student that would allow a reasonable person in the school

community, who does not have personal knowledge of the relevant circumstances, to identify the student with reasonable certainty; or

(g) Information requested by a person who the educational agency or institution reasonably believes knows the identity of the student to whom the education record relates.

[Authority: 20 u.s.c. 1232g]

"RECORD" means any information recorded in any way, including, but not limited to, handwriting, print, computer media, video or audio tape, film, microfilm, and microfiche.

[Authority: 20 u.s.c. 1232g]

"SECRETARY" means the Secretary of the U.S. Department of Education or an official or employee of the Department of Education acting for the Secretary under a delegation of authority.

[Authority: 20 u.s.c. 1232g]

"STUDENT," except as otherwise specifically provided in this part, means any individual who is or has been in attendance at an educational agency or institution and regarding whom the agency or institution maintains education records.

[Authority: 20 u.s.c. 1232g(a)(6)]

§ 99.4 WHAT ARE THE RIGHTS OF PARENTS?

An educational agency or institution shall give full rights under the *Act* to either parent, unless the agency or institution has been provided with evidence that there is a court order, state statute, or legally binding document relating to such matters as divorce, separation, or custody that specifically revokes these rights.
[Authority: 20 u.s.c. 1232g]

§ 99.5 WHAT ARE THE RIGHTS OF STUDENTS?

(a)(1) When a student becomes an eligible student, the rights accorded to, and consent required of, parents under this part transfer from the parents to the student.

(2) Nothing in this section prevents an educational agency or institution from disclosing education records, or personally identifiable information from education records, to a parent without the prior written consent of an eligible student if the disclosure meets the conditions in §99.31(a)(8), §99.31(a)(10), §99.31(a)(15), or any other provision in §99.31(a).

(b) The *Act* and this part do not prevent educational agencies or institutions from giving students rights in addition to those given to parents.

(c) An individual who is or has been a student at an education institution and who applies for admission at another component of that institution does not have rights under this part with respect to records maintained by that other component, including records maintained in connection with the student's application for admission, unless the student is accepted and attends that other component of the institution.

[Authority: 20 u.s.c. 1232g(d)]

§ 99.7 WHAT MUST AN EDUCATIONAL AGENCY OR INSTITUTION INCLUDE IN ITS ANNUAL NOTIFICATION?

(a)(1) Each educational agency or institution shall annually notify parents of students currently in attendance, or eligible students currently in attendance, of their rights under the *Act* and this part.

(2) The notice must inform parents or eligible students that they have the right to—

(i) Inspect and review the student's education records;

(ii) Seek amendment of the student's education records that the parent or eligible student believes to be inaccurate, misleading, or otherwise in violation of the student's privacy rights;

(iii) Consent to disclosures of personally identifiable information contained in the student's education records, except to the extent that the *Act* and § 99.31 authorize disclosure without consent; and

(iv) File with the Department a complaint under § 99.63 and § 99.64 concerning alleged failures by the educational agency or institution to comply with the requirements of the act and this part.

(3) The notice must include all of the following:

(i) The procedure for exercising the right to inspect and review education records.

(ii) The procedure for requesting amendment of records under § 99.20.

(iii) If the educational agency or institution has a policy of disclosing education records under § 99.31(a)(1), a specification of criteria for determining who constitutes a school official and what constitutes a legitimate educational interest.

(b) An educational agency or institution may provide this notice by any means that are reasonably likely to inform the parents or eligible students of their rights.

(1) An educational agency or institution shall effectively notify parents or eligible students who are disabled.

(2) An agency or institution of elementary or secondary education shall effectively notify parents who have a primary or home language other than English.

(Approved by the Office of Management and Budget under control number 1880–0508)

[Authority 20 U.S.C. 1232g(e) and (f)]

§ 99.8 WHAT PROVISIONS APPLY TO RECORDS OF A LAW ENFORCEMENT UNIT?

(a)(1) "Law enforcement unit" means any individual, office, department, division, or other component of an educational agency or institution, such as a unit of commissioned police officers or non-commissioned security guards, that is officially authorized or designated by that agency or institution to—

(i) Enforce any local, state, or federal law, or refer to appropriate authorities a matter for enforcement of any local, state, or federal law against any individual or organization other than the agency or institution itself; or

(ii) Maintain the physical security and safety of the agency or institution.

(2) A component of an educational agency or institution does not lose its status as a "law enforcement unit" if it also performs other, non-law enforcement functions for the agency or institution, including investigation of incidents or conduct that constitutes or leads to a disciplinary action or proceedings against the student.

(b)(1) Records of law enforcement unit means those records, files, documents, and other materials that are—

(i) Created by a law enforcement unit;
(ii) Created for a law enforcement purpose; and
(iii) Maintained by the law enforcement unit.

(2) Records of law enforcement unit does not mean—

(i) Records created by a law enforcement unit for a law enforcement purpose that are maintained by a component of the educational agency or institution other than the law enforcement unit; or
(ii) Records created and maintained by a law enforcement unit exclusively for a non-law enforcement purpose, such as a disciplinary action or proceeding conducted by the educational agency or institution.

(c)(1) Nothing in the *Act* prohibits an educational agency or institution from contacting its law enforcement unit, orally or in writing, for the purpose of asking that unit to investigate a possible violation of, or to enforce, any local, state, or federal law.

(2) Education records, and personally identifiable information contained in education records, do not lose their status as education records and remain subject to the *Act*, including the disclosure provisions of § 99.30, while in possession of the law enforcement unit.

(d) The *Act* neither requires nor prohibits the dis-closure by any educational agency or institution of its law enforcement unit records.

[Authority: 20 u.s.c. 1232g(a)(4)(B)(ii)]

Subpart B—What Are the Rights of Inspection and Review of Education Records?

§ 99.10 WHAT RIGHTS EXIST FOR A PARENT OR ELIGIBLE STUDENT TO INSPECT AND REVIEW EDUCATION RECORDS?

(a) Except as limited under § 99.12, a parent or eligible student must be given the opportunity to inspect and review the student's education records.

This provision applies to—

(1) Any educational agency or institution; and

(2) Any state educational agency (SEA) and its   components.

> (i) For the purposes of subpart B of this part, an SEA and its components constitute an educational agency or institution.

> (ii) An SEA and its components are subject to subpart B of this part if the SEA maintains education records on students who are or have been in attendance at any school of an educational agency or institution subject to the *Act* and this part.

(b) The educational agency or institution, or SEA or its component, shall comply with a request for access to records within a reasonable period of time, but not more than 45 days after it has received the request.

(c) The educational agency or institution, or SEA or its component, shall respond to reasonable requests for explanations and interpretations of the records.

(d) If circumstances effectively prevent the parent or eligible student from exercising the right to inspect and review the student's education records, the educational agency or institution, or SEA or its component, shall—

(1) Provide the parent or eligible student with a copy of the records requested; or

(2) Make other arrangements for the parent or eligible student to inspect and review the requested records.

(e) The educational agency or institution, or SEA or its component, shall not destroy any education records if there is an outstanding request to inspect and review the records under this section.

(f) While an education agency or institution is not required to give an eligible student access to treatment records under paragraph (b)(4) of the definition of "Education records" in § 99.3, the student may have those records reviewed by a physician or other appropriate professional of the student's choice.

[Authority: 20 u.s.c. 1232g(a)(1)(A) and (B)]

§ 99.11 MAY AN EDUCATIONAL AGENCY OR INSTITUTION CHARGE A FEE FOR COPIES OF EDUCATION RECORDS?

(a) Unless the imposition of a fee effectively prevents a parent or eligible student from exercising the right to inspect and review the student's education records, an educational agency or institution may charge a fee for a copy of an education record which is made for the parent or eligible student.

(b) An educational agency or institution may not charge a fee to search for or to retrieve the education records of a student.

[Authority: 20 u.s.c. 1232g(a)(1)]

§ 99.12 WHAT LIMITATIONS EXIST ON THE RIGHT TO INSPECT AND REVIEW RECORDS?

(a) If the education records of a student contain information on more than one student, the parent or eligible student may inspect and review or be informed of only the specific information about that student.

(b) A postsecondary institution does not have to permit a student to inspect and review education records that are:

(1) Financial records, including any information those records contain, of his or her parents;

(2) Confidential letters and confidential statements of recommendation placed in the education records of the student before January 1, 1975, as long as the statements are used only for the purposes for which they were specifically intended; and

(3) Confidential letters and confidential statements of recommendation placed in the student's education records after January 1, 1975, if:

(i) The student has waived his or her right to inspect and review those letters and statements; and

(ii) Those letters and statements are related to the student's:

(A) Admission to an education institution;
(B) Application for employment; or
(C) Receipt of an honor or honorary recognition.

(c)(1) A waiver under paragraph (b)(3)(i) of this section is valid only if:

(i) The educational agency or institution does not require the waiver as a condition for admission to or receipt of a service or benefit from the agency or institution; and

(ii) The waiver is made in writing and signed by the student, regardless of age.

(2) If a student has waived his or her rights under paragraph (b)(3)(i) of this section, the education institution shall:

(i) Give the student, on request, the names of the individuals who provided the letters and statements of recommendation; and

(ii) Use the letters and statements of recommendation only for the purpose for which they were intended.

(3)(i) A waiver under paragraph (b)(3)(i) of this section may be revoked with respect to any actions occurring after the revocation.

(ii) A revocation under paragraph (c)(3)(i) of this section must be in writing.

[Authority: 20 u.s.c. 1232g(a)(1)(A), (B), (C), and (D)]

Subpart C—What Are the Procedures for Amending Education Records?

§ 99.20 HOW CAN A PARENT OR ELIGIBLE STUDENT REQUEST AMENDMENT OF THE STUDENT'S EDUCATION RECORDS?

(a) If a parent or eligible student believes the education records relating to the student contain information that is inaccurate, misleading, or in violation of the student's rights of privacy, he or she may ask the educational agency or institution to amend the record.

(b) The educational agency or institution shall decide whether to amend the record as requested within a reasonable time after the agency or institution receives the request.

(c) If the educational agency or institution decides not to amend the record as requested, it shall inform the parent or eligible student of its decision and of his or her right to a hearing under § 99.21.

[Authority: 20 u.s.c. 1232g(a)(2)]

§ 99.21 UNDER WHAT CONDITIONS DOES A PARENT OR ELIGIBLE STUDENT HAVE THE RIGHT TO A HEARING?

(a) An educational agency or institution shall give a parent or eligible student, on request, an opportunity for a hearing to challenge the content of the student's education records on the grounds that the information contained in the education records is inaccurate, misleading, or in violation of the privacy rights of the student.

(b)(1) If, as a result of the hearing, the educational agency or institution decides that the information is inaccurate, misleading, or otherwise in violation of the privacy rights of the student, it shall:

(i) Amend the record accordingly; and

(ii) Inform the parent or eligible student of the amendment in writing.

(2) If, as a result of the hearing, the educational agency or institution decides that the information in the education record is not inaccurate, misleading, or otherwise in violation of the privacy rights of the student, it shall inform the parent or eligible student of the right to place a statement in the record commenting on the contested information in the record or stating why he or she disagrees with the decision of the agency or institution, or both.

(c) If an educational agency or institution places a statement in the education records of a student under paragraph (b)(2) of this section, the agency or institution shall:

(1) Maintain the statement with the contested part of the record for as long as the record is maintained; and

(2) Disclose the statement whenever it discloses the portion of the record to which the statement relates.

[Authority: 20 u.s.c. 1232g(a)(2)]

§ 99.22 WHAT MINIMUM REQUIREMENTS EXIST FOR THE CONDUCT OF A HEARING?

The hearing required by § 99.21 must meet, at a minimum, the following requirements:

(a) The educational agency or institution shall hold the hearing within a reasonable time after it has received the request for the hearing from the parent or eligible student.

(b) The educational agency or institution shall give the parent or eligible student notice of the date, time, and place, reasonably in advance of the hearing.

(c) The hearing may be conducted by any individual, including an official of the educational agency or institution, who does not have a direct interest in the outcome of the hearing.

(d) The educational agency or institution shall give the parent or eligible student a full and fair opportunity to present evidence relevant to the issues raised under § 99.21. The parent or eligible student may, at their own expense, be assisted or represented by one or more individuals of his or her own choice, including an attorney.

(e) The educational agency or institution shall make its decision in writing within a reasonable period of time after the hearing.

(f) The decision must be based solely on the evidence presented at the hearing, and must include a summary of the evidence and the reasons for the decision.

[Authority: 20 u.s.c. 1232g(a)(2)]

Subpart D—May an Educational Agency or Institution Disclose Personally Identifiable Information from Education Records?

§ 99.30 UNDER WHAT CONDITIONS IS PRIOR CONSENT REQUIRED TO DISCLOSE INFORMATION?

(a) The parent or eligible student shall provide a signed and dated written consent before an educational agency or institution discloses personally identifiable information from the student's education records, except as provided in § 99.31.

(b) The written consent must:

(1) Specify the records that may be disclosed;
(2) State the purpose of the disclosure; and
(3) Identify the party or class of parties to whom the disclosure may be made.

(c) When a disclosure is made under paragraph (a) of this section:

(1) If a parent or eligible student so requests, the educational agency or institution shall provide him or her with a copy of the records disclosed; and
(2) If the parent of a student who is not an eligible student so requests, the agency or institution shall provide the student with a copy of the records disclosed.

(d) "Signed and dated written consent" under this part may include a record and signature in electronic form that—

(1) Identifies and authenticates a particular person as the source of the electronic consent; and
(2) Indicates such person's approval of the information contained in the electronic consent.

[Authority: 20 u.s.c. 1232g(b)(1) and (b)(2)(A)]

§ 99.31 UNDER WHAT CONDITIONS IS PRIOR CONSENT NOT REQUIRED TO DISCLOSE INFORMATION?

(a) An educational agency or institution may disclose personally identifiable information from an education record of a student without the consent required by § 99.30 if the disclosure meets one or more of the following conditions:

(1)(i)(A) The disclosure is to other school officials, including teachers, within the agency or institution whom the agency or institution has determined to have legitimate educational interests.

(B) A contractor, consultant, volunteer, or other party to whom an agency or institution has outsourced institutional services or functions may be considered a school official under this paragraph provided that the outside party—

(1) Performs an institutional service or function for which the agency or institution would otherwise use employees;

(2) Is under the direct control of the agency or institution with respect to the use and maintenance of education records; and

(3) Is subject to the requirements of §99.33(a) governing the use and redisclosure of personally identifiable information from education records.

(ii) An educational agency or institution must use reasonable methods to ensure that school officials obtain access to only those education records in which they have legitimate educational interests. An educational agency or institution that does not use physical or technological access controls must ensure that its administrative policy for controlling access to education records is effective and that it remains in compliance with the legitimate educational interest requirement in paragraph (a)(1)(i)(A) of this section.

(2) The disclosure is, subject to the requirements of § 99.34, to officials of another school, school system, or institution of postsecondary education where the student seeks or intends to enroll, or where the student is already enrolled so long as the disclosure is for purposes related to the student's enrollment or transfer.

Note: Section 4155(b) of the No Child Left Behind Act of 2001, 20 U.S.C. 7165(b), requires each State to assure the Secretary of Education that it has a procedure in place to facilitate the transfer of disciplinary records with respect to a suspension or expulsion of a student by a local educational agency to any private or public elementary or secondary school in which the student is subsequently enrolled or seeks, intends, or is instructed to enroll.

(3) The disclosure is, subject to the requirements of § 99.35, to authorized representatives of—

(i) The Comptroller General of the United States;
(ii) The Attorney General of the United States;
(iii) The Secretary; or
(iv) State and local educational authorities.

(4)(i) The disclosure is in connection with financial aid for which the student has applied or which the student has received, if the information is necessary for such purposes as to:

(A) Determine eligibility for the aid;
(B) Determine the amount of the aid;
(C) Determine the conditions for the aid; or
(D) Enforce the terms and conditions of the aid.

(ii) As used in paragraph (a)(4)(i) of this section, "financial aid" means a payment of funds provided to an individual (or a payment in kind of tangible or intangible property to the individual) that is conditioned on the individual's attendance at an educational agency or institution.

[Authority: 20 u.s.c. 1232g(b)(1)(D)]

(5)(i) The disclosure is to state and local officials or authorities to whom this information is specifically-

(A) Allowed to be reported or disclosed pursuant to a state statute adopted before November 19, 1974, if the allowed reporting or disclosure concerns the juvenile justice system and the system's ability to effectively serve the student whose records are released;or
(B) Allowed to be reported or disclosed pursuant to a state statute adopted after November 19, 1974, subject to the requirements of § 99.38.

(ii) Paragraph (a)(5)(1) of this section does not prevent a state from further limiting the number or type of state or local officials to whom disclosures may be made under that paragraph.

(6)(i) The disclosure is to organizations conducting studies for, or on behalf of, educational agencies or institutions to:

(A) Develop, validate, or administer predictive tests;
(B) Administer student aid programs; or
(C) Improve instruction.

(ii) An educational agency or institution may disclose information
under paragraph (a)(6)(i) of this section only if:

(A) The study is conducted in a manner that does not permit personal identification of parents and students by individuals other
than representatives of the organization that have legitimate interests in the information;
(B) The information is destroyed when no longer needed for the purposes for which the study was conducted.
(C) The educational agency or institution enters into a written agreement with the organization that—

(1) Specifies the purpose, scope, and duration of the study or studies and the information to be disclosed;
(2) Requires the organization to use personally identifiable information from education records only to meet the purpose or
purposes of the study as stated in the written agreement;
(3) Requires the organization to conduct the study in a manner
that does not permit personal identification of parents and students, as defined in this part, by anyone other than representatives of the organization with legitimate interests; and
(4) Requires the organization to destroy or return to the educational agency or institution all personally identifiable information when the information is no longer needed for the purposes
for which the study was conducted and specifies the time period in which the information must be returned or destroyed.

(iii) An educational agency or institution is not required to initiate a
study or agree with or endorse the conclusions or results of the study.
(iv) If this Office determines that a third party outside the educational agency or institution to whom information is disclosed un-

der this paragraph (a)(6) violates paragraph (a)(6)(ii)(B) of this section, the educational agency or institution may not allow that third party access to personally identifiable information from education records for at least five years.

(v) For the purposes of paragraph (a)(6) of this section, the term "organization" includes, but is not limited to, federal, state, and local agencies, and independent organizations.

(7) The disclosure is to accrediting organizations to carry out their accrediting functions.

(8) The disclosure is to parents, as defined in § 99.3, of a dependent student, as defined in section 152 of the Internal Revenue Code of 1986.

(9)(i) The disclosure is to comply with a judicial order or lawfully issued subpoena.

(ii) The educational agency or institution may disclose information under paragraph (a)(9)(i) of this section only if the agency or institution makes a reasonable effort to notify the parent or eligible student of the order or subpoena in advance of compliance, so that the parent or eligible student may seek protective action, unless the disclosure is in compliance with—

(A) A federal grand jury subpoena and the court has ordered that the existence or the contents of the subpoena or the information furnished in response to the subpoena not be disclosed;

(B) Any other subpoena issued for a law enforcement purpose and the court or other issuing agency has ordered that the existence or the contents of the subpoena or the information furnished in response to the subpoena not be disclosed; or

(C) An *ex parte* court order obtained by the United States Attorney General (or designee not lower than an Assistant Attorney General) concerning investigations or prosecutions of an offense listed in 18 U.S.C. 2332b(g)(5)(B) or an act of domestic or international terrorism as defined in 18 U.S.C. 2331.

(iii)(A) If an educational agency or institution initiates legal action against a parent or student, the educational agency or institution may disclose to the court, without a court order or subpoena, the education records of the student that are relevant for the educational agency or institution to proceed with the legal action as plaintiff.

(B) If a parent or eligible student initiates legal action against an educational agency or institution, the educational agency or institution may disclose to the court, without a court order or subpoena, the student's education records that are relevant for the educational agency or institution to defend itself.

(10) The disclosure is in connection with a health or safety emergency, under the conditions described in § 99.36.

(11) The disclosure is information the educational agency or institution has designated as "directory information," under the conditions described in § 99.37.

(12) The disclosure is to the parent of a student who is not an eligible student or to the student.

(13) The disclosure, subject to the requirements in § 99.39, is to a victim of an alleged perpetrator of a crime of violence or a non-forcible sex offense. The disclosure may only include the final results of the disciplinary proceeding conducted by the institution of postsecondary education with respect to that alleged crime or offense. The institution may disclose the final results of the disciplinary proceeding, regardless of whether the institution concluded a violation was committed.

(14)(i) The disclosure, subject to the requirements in § 99.39, is in connection with a disciplinary proceeding at an institution of postsecondary education. The institution must not disclose the final results of the disciplinary proceeding unless it determines that—

(A) The student is an alleged perpetrator of a crime of violence or non-forcible sex offense; and

(B) With respect to the allegation made against him or her, the student has committed a violation of the institution's rules or policies.

(ii) The institution may not disclose the name of any other student, including a victim or witness, without the prior written consent of the other student.

(iii) This section applies only to disciplinary proceedings in which the final results were reached on or after October 7, 1998.

(15)(i) The disclosure is to a parent of a student at an institution of post-secondary education regarding the student's violation of any federal, state, or local law, or of any rule or policy of the institution, governing the use or possession of alcohol or a controlled substance if—

    (A) The institution determines that the student has committed a disciplinary violation with respect to that use or possession; and

    (B) The student is under the age of 21 at the time of the disclosure to the parent.

    (ii) Paragraph (a)(15) of this section does not supersede any provision of state law that prohibits an institution of postsecondary education from disclosing information.

(16) The disclosure concerns sex offenders and other individuals required to register under section 170101 of the Violent Crime Control and Law Enforcement Act of 1994, 42 U.S.C. 14071, and the information was provided to the educational agency or institution under 42 U.S.C. 14071 and applicable federal guidelines.

    (b)(1) De-identified records and information. An educational agency or institution, or a party that has received education records or information from education records under this part, may release the records or information without the consent required by §99.30 after the removal of all personally identifiable information provided that the educational agency or institution or other party has made a reasonable determination that a student's identity is not personally identifiable, whether through single or multiple releases, and taking into account other reasonably available information.

    (2) An educational agency or institution, or a party that has received education records or information from education records under this part, may release de-identified student level data from education records for the purpose of education research by attaching a code to each record that may allow the recipient to match information received from the same source, provided that—

(i) An educational agency or institution or other party that releases de-identified data under paragraph (b)(2) of this section does not disclose any information about how it generates and assigns a record code, or that would allow a recipient to identify a student based on a record code;

(ii) The record code is used for no purpose other than identifying a de-identified record for purposes of education research and cannot be used to ascertain personally identifiable information about a student; and

(iii) The record code is not based on a student's social security number or other personal information.

(c) An educational agency or institution must use reasonable methods to identify and authenticate the identity of parents, students, school officials, and any other parties to whom the agency or institution discloses personally identifiable information from education records.

(d) Paragraphs (a) and (b) of this section do not require an educational agency or institution or any other party to disclose education records or information from education records to any party except for parties under paragraph (a)(12) of this section.

[Authority: 20 u.s.c. 1232g(a)(5)(A), (b), (h), (i), and (j)]

§ 99.32 WHAT RECORDKEEPING REQUIREMENTS EXIST CONCERNING REQUESTS AND DISCLOSURES?

(a)(1) An educational agency or institution must maintain a record of each request for access to and each disclosure of personally identifiable information from the education records of each student , as well as the names of State and local educational authorities and Federal officials and agencies listed in §99.31(a)(3) that may make further disclosures of personally identifiable information from the student's education records without consent under §99.33(b).

(2) The agency or institution shall maintain the record with the education records of the student as long as the records are maintained.

(3) For each request or disclosure the record must include:

(i) The parties who have requested or received personally identifiable information from the education records; and

(ii) The legitimate interests the parties had in re-questing or obtaining the information.

(4) An educational agency or institution must obtain a copy of the re-cord of further disclosures maintained under paragraph (b)(2) of this section and make it available in response to a parent's or eligible stu-dent's request to review the record required under paragraph (a)(1) of this section.

(5) An educational agency or institution must record the following infor-mation when it discloses personally identifiable information from education records under the health or safety emergency exception in §99.31(a)(10) and §99.36:

(i) The articulable and significant threat to the health or safety of a student or other individuals that formed the basis for the disclo-sure; and

(ii) The parties to whom the agency or institution disclosed the infor-mation.

(b)(1) Except as provided in paragraph (b)(2) of this section, if an education-al agency or institution discloses personally identifiable information from education records with the understanding authorized under §99.33(b), the record of the disclosure required under this section must include:

(i) The names of the additional parties to which the receiving party may disclose the information on behalf of the educational agency or institution; and

(ii) The legitimate interests under §99.31 which each of the additional parties has in requesting or obtaining the information.

(2)(i) A State or local educational authority or Federal official or agency listed in §99.31(a)(3) that makes further disclosures of information from education records under §99.33(b) must record the names of the additional parties to which it discloses information on behalf of an educational agency or institution and their legitimate interests in the information under §99.31 if the information was received from:

(A) An educational agency or institution that has not recorded the further disclosures under paragraph (b)(1) of this section; or

(B) Another State or local educational authority or Federal official or agency listed in §99.31(a)(3).

(ii) A State or local educational authority or Federal official or agency that records further disclosures of information under paragraph (b)(2)(i) of this section may maintain the record by the student's class, school, district, or other appropriate grouping rather than by the name of the student.

(iii) Upon request of an educational agency or institution, a State or local educational authority or Federal official or agency listed in §99.31(a)(3) that maintains a record of further disclosures under paragraph (b)(2)(i) of this section must provide a copy of the record of further disclosures to the educational agency or institution within a reasonable period of time not to exceed 30 days.

(c) The following parties may inspect the record relating to each student:

(1) The parent or eligible student.

(2) The school official or his or her assistants who are responsible for the custody of the records.

(3) Those parties authorized in § 99.3 1 (a)(1) and (3) for the purposes of auditing the recordkeeping procedures of the educational agency or institution.

(d) Paragraph (a) of this section does not apply if the request was from, or the disclosure was to:

(1) The parent or eligible student;

(2) A school official under § 99.3 1 (a)(1);

(3) A party with written consent from the parent or eligible student;

(4) A party seeking directory information; or

(5) A party seeking or receiving the records in accordance with §99.31(a)(9)(ii)(A) through (C).

(Approved by the Office of Management and Budget under control number 1880–0508)

[Authority: 20 u.s.c. 1232g(b)(1) and (b)(4)(A)]

(a)(1) An educational agency or institution may disclose personally identifiable information from an education record only on the condition that the party to whom the information is disclosed will not disclose the information to any other party without the prior consent of the parent or eligible student.

(2) The officers, employees, and agents of a party that receives information under paragraph (a)(1) of this section may use the information, but only for the purposes for which the disclosure was made.

(b)(1) Paragraph (a) of this section does not prevent an educational agency or institution from disclosing personally identifiable information with the understanding that the party receiving the information may make further disclosures of the information on behalf of the educational agency or institution if:

(i) The disclosures meet the requirements of § 99.31; and

(ii)(A) The educational agency or institution has complied with the requirements of § 99.32(b); or

(B) A State or local educational authority or Federal official or agency listed in §99.31(a)(3) has complied with the requirements of §99.32(b)(2).

(2) A party that receives a court order or lawfully issued subpoena and rediscloses personally identifiable information from education records on behalf of an educational agency or institution in response to that order or subpoena under §99.31(a)(9) must provide the notification required under §99.31(a)(9)(ii).

(c) Paragraph (a) of this section does not apply to disclosures under §§99.31(a)(8), (9), (11), (12), (14), (15), and (16), and to information that postsecondary institutions are required to disclose under the Jeanne Clery Disclosure of Campus Security Policy and Campus Crime Statistics Act, 20 U.S.C.

1092(f) (Clery Act), to the accuser and accused regarding the outcome of any campus disciplinary proceeding brought alleging a sexual offense.

(d) An educational agency or institution must inform a party to whom disclosure is made of the requirements of paragraph (a) of this section except for disclosures made under §§99.31(a)(8), (9), (11), (12), (14), (15), and (16), and to information that postsecondary institutions are required to disclose under the Clery Act to the accuser and accused regarding the outcome of any campus disciplinary proceeding brought alleging a sexual offense.

(e) If this Office determines that a third party outside the educational agency or institution improperly rediscloses personally identifiable information from education records in violation of this section, or fails to provide the notification required under paragraph (b)(2) of this section, the educational agency or institution may not allow that third party access to personally identifiable information from education records for at least five years.

[Authority: 20 u.s.c. 1232g(b)(4)(B)]

§ 99.34 WHAT CONDITIONS APPLY TO DISCLOSURE OF INFORMATION TO OTHER EDUCATIONAL AGENCIES OR INSTITUTIONS?

(a) An educational agency or institution that discloses an education record under § 99.31(a)(2) shall:

(1) Make a reasonable attempt to notify the parent or eligible student at the last known address of the parent or eligible student, unless:

(i) The disclosure is initiated by the parent or eligible student; or

(ii) The annual notification of the agency or institution under § 99.7 includes a notice that the agency or institution forwards education records to other agencies or institutions that have requested the records and in which the student seeks or intends to enroll or is already enrolled so long as the disclosure is for purposes related to the student's enrollment or transfer:

(2) Give the parent or eligible student, upon request, a copy of the record that was disclosed; and

(3) Give the parent or eligible student, upon request, an opportunity for a hearing under Subpart C.

(b) An educational agency or institution may disclose an education record of a student in attendance to another educational agency or institution if:

(1) The student is enrolled in or receives services from the other agency or institution; and

(2) The disclosure meets the requirements of paragraph (a) of this section.

[Authority: 20 u.s.c. 1232g(b)(1)(B)]

§ 99.35 WHAT CONDITIONS APPLY TO DISCLOSURE OF INFORMATION FOR FEDERAL OR STATE PROGRAM PURPOSES?

(a)(1) Authorized representatives of the officials or agencies headed by officials listed in §99.31(a)(3) may have access to education records in connection with an audit or evaluation of federal or state supported education programs, or for the enforcement of or compliance with federal legal requirements that relate to those programs.

(2) Authority for an agency or official listed in §99.31(a)(3) to conduct an audit, evaluation, or compliance or enforcement activity is not conferred by the Act or this part and must be established under other Federal, State, or local authority.

(b) Information that is collected under paragraph (a) of this section must:

(1) Be protected in a manner that does not permit personal identification of individuals by anyone other than the officials or agencies headed by officials referred to in paragraph (a) of this section, except that those officials and agencies may make further disclosures of personally identifiable information from education records on behalf of the educational agency or institution in accordance with the requirements of §99.33(b); and

(2) Be destroyed when no longer needed for the purposes listed in paragraph (a) of this section.

(c) Paragraph (b) of this section does not apply if:

(1) The parent or eligible student has given written consent for the disclosure under § 99.30; or

(2) The collection of personally identifiable information is specifically authorized by federal law.

[Authority: 20 u.s.c. 1232g(b)(3)]

§ 99.36 WHAT CONDITIONS APPLY TO DISCLOSURE OF INFORMATION IN HEALTH AND SAFETY EMERGENCIES?

(a) An educational agency or institution may disclose personally identifiable information from an education record to appropriate parties, including parents of an eligible student, in connection with an emergency if knowledge of the information is necessary to protect the health or safety of the student or other individuals.

(b) Nothing in the *Act* or this part shall prevent an educational agency or institution from-

(1) Including in the education records of a student appropriate information concerning disciplinary action taken against the student for conduct that posed a significant risk to the safety or well-being of that student, other students, or other members of the school community;

(2) Disclosing appropriate information maintained under paragraph (b)(1) of this section to teachers and school officials within the agency or institution who the agency or institution has determined have legitimate educational interests in the behavior of the student; or

(3) Disclosing appropriate information maintained under paragraph (b)(1) of this section to teachers and school officials in other schools who have been determined to have legitimate educational interests in the behavior of the student.

(c) In making a determination under paragraph (a) of this section, an educational agency or institution may take into account the totality of the circumstances pertaining to a threat to the health or safety of a student or other individuals. If the educational agency or institution determines that there is an articulable and significant threat to the health or safety of a student or other individuals, it may disclose information from education records to any person whose knowledge of the information is necessary to protect the health or safety of the student or other individuals. If, based on the information available at the time of the determination, there is a rational basis for the determination, the Department will not substitute its judgment for that of the educational agency or institution in evaluating the circumstances and making its determination.

[Authority: 20 u.s.c. 1232g(b)(1)(I) and (h)]

§ 99.37 WHAT CONDITIONS APPLY TO DISCLOSING DIRECTORY INFORMATION?

(a) An educational agency or institution may disclose directory information if it has given public notice to parents of students in attendance and eligible students in attendance at the agency or institution of:

    (1) The types of personally identifiable information that the agency or institution has designated as directory information;

    (2) A parent's or eligible student's right to refuse to let the agency or institution designate any or all of those types of information about the student as directory information; and

    (3) The period of time within which a parent or eligible student has to notify the agency or institution in writing that he or she does not want any or all of those types of information about the student designated as directory information.

(b) An educational agency or institution may disclose directory information about former students without meeting the conditions in paragraph (a) of this section. However, the agency or institution must continue to honor any valid request to opt out of the disclosure of directory information made while a student was in attendance unless the student rescinds the opt out request.

(c) A parent or eligible student may not use the right under paragraph (a)(2) of this section to opt out of directory information disclosures to prevent an educational agency or institution from disclosing or requiring a student to disclose the student's name, identifier, or institutional email address in a class in which the student is enrolled.

(d) An educational agency or institution may not disclose or confirm directory information without meeting the written consent requirements in §99.30 if a student's social security number or other non-directory information is used alone or combined with other data elements to identify or help identify the student or the student's records.

[Authority: 20 u.s.c. 1232g(a)(5)(A) and (B)]

§ 99.38 WHAT CONDITIONS APPLY TO DISCLOSURE OF INFORMATION AS PERMITTED BY STATE STATUTE ADOPTED AFTER NOVEMBER 19, 1974 CONCERNING THE JUVENILE JUSTICE SYSTEM?

(a) If reporting or disclosure allowed by state statute concerns the juvenile justice system and the system's ability to effectively serve, prior to adjudication, the student whose records are released, an educational agency or institution may disclose education records under § 99.31(a)(5)(i)(B).

(b) The officials and authorities to whom the records are disclosed shall certify in writing to the educational agency or institution that the information will not be disclosed to any other party, except as provided under state law, without the prior written consent of the parent of the student.

[Authority: 20 u.s.c. 1232g(b)(1)(J)]

§ 99.39 WHAT DEFINITIONS APPLY TO THE NONCONSENSUAL DISCLOSURE OF RECORDS BY POSTSECONDARY EDUCATIONAL INSTITUTIONS IN CONNECTION WITH DISCIPLINARY PROCEEDINGS CONCERNING CRIMES OF VIOLENCE OR NON-FORCIBLE SEX OFFENSES?

As used in this part:

ALLEGED PERPETRATOR OF A CRIME OF VIOLENCE is a student who is alleged to have committed acts that would, if proven, constitute any of the following offenses or attempts to commit the following offenses that are defined in appendix A to this part:

- Arson
- Assault offenses
- Burglary
- Criminal homicide—manslaughter by negligence
- Criminal homicide—murder and nonnegligent manslaughter
- Destruction/damage/vandalism of property
- Kidnapping/abduction
- Robbery
- Forcible sex offenses

ALLEGED PERPETRATOR OF A NONFORCIBLE SEX OFFENSE means a student who is alleged to have committed acts that, if proven, would constitute statutory rape or incest. These offenses are defined in Appendix A to this part.

FINAL RESULTS means a decision or determination, made by an honor court or council, committee, commission, or other entity authorized to resolve disciplinary matters within the institution. The disclosure of final results must include only the name of the student, the violation committed, and any sanction imposed by the institution against the student.

SANCTION IMPOSED means a description of the disciplinary action taken by the institution, the date of its imposition, and its duration.

VIOLATION COMMITTED means the institutional rules or code sections that were violated and any essential findings supporting the institution's conclusion that the violation was committed.

[Authority: 20 u.s.c. 1232g(b)(6)]

Subpart E—What Are the Enforcement Procedures?

§ 99.60 WHAT FUNCTIONS HAS THE SECRETARY DELEGATED TO THE OFFICE AND TO THE OFFICE OF ADMINISTRATIVE LAW JUDGES?

(a) For the purposes of this subpart, "Office" means the Family Policy Compliance Office, U.S. Department of Education.

(b) The Secretary designates the Office to:

(1) Investigate, process, and review complaints and violations under the *Act* and this part; and

(2) Provide technical assistance to ensure compliance with the *Act* and this part.

(c) The Secretary designates the Office of Administrative Law Judges to act as the Review Board required under the *Act* to enforce the *Act* with respect to all applicable programs. The term "applicable program" is defined in section 400 of the *General Education Provisions Act*.

[Authority: 20 u.s.c. 1232g(f) and (g), 1234]

§ 99.61 WHAT RESPONSIBILITY DOES AN EDUCATIONAL AGENCY OR INSTITUTION HAVE CONCERNING CONFLICT WITH STATE OR LOCAL LAWS?

If an educational agency or institution determines that it cannot comply with the *Act* or this part due to a conflict with state or local law, it shall notify the Office within 45 days, giving the text and citation of the conflicting law.

[Authority: 20 u.s.c. 1232g(f)]

§ 99.62 WHAT INFORMATION MUST AN EDUCATIONAL AGENCY OR INSTITUTION SUBMIT TO THE OFFICE?

The Office may require an educational agency or institution to submit reports, information on policies and procedures, annual notifications, training materials, and other information necessary to carry out its enforcement responsibilities under the Act or this part.

[Authority: 20 u.s.c. 1232g(f) and (g)]

§ 99.63 WHERE ARE COMPLAINTS FILED?

A parent or eligible student may file a written complaint with the Office regarding an alleged violation under the *Act* and this part. The Office's address is: Family Policy Compliance Office, U.S. Department of Education, 400 Maryland Avenue, SW, Washington, D.C. 20202–4605.

[Authority: 20 u.s.c. 1232g(g)]

§ 99.64 WHAT IS THE INVESTIGATION PROCEDURE?

(a) A complaint filed under § 99.63 must contain specific allegations of fact giving reasonable cause to believe that a violation of the *Act* or this part has occurred. A complaint does not have to allege that a violation is based on a policy or practice of the educational agency or institution.

(b) The Office investigates a timely complaint filed by a parent or eligible student, or conducts its own investigation when no complaint has been filed or a complaint has been withdrawn, to determine whether an educational agency or institution has failed to comply with a provision of the Act or this part. If the Office determines that an educational agency or institution has failed to comply with a provision of the Act or this part, it may also determine whether the failure to comply is based on a policy or practice of the agency or institution.

(c) A timely complaint is defined as an allegation of a violation of the *Act* that is submitted to the Office within 180 days of the date of the alleged violation or of the date that the complainant knew or reasonably should have known of the alleged violation.

(d) The Office may extend the time limit in this section for good cause shown.

[Authority: 20 u.s.c. 1232g(f)]

§ 99.65 WHAT IS THE CONTENT OF THE NOTICE OF INVESTIGATION ISSUED BY THE OFFICE?

(a) The Office notifies the complainant, if any, and the educational agency or institution in writing if it initiates an investigation of a complaint under § 99.64(b). The notice to the educational agency or institution-

  (1) Includes the substance of the alleged violation; and

  (2) Directs the agency or institution to submit a written response and other relevant information, as set forth in §99.62, within a specified period of time, including information about its policies and practices regarding education records.

(b) The Office notifies the complainant if it does not initiate an investigation of a complaint because the complaint fails to meet the requirements of § 99.64.

[Authority: 20 u.s.c. 1232g(g)]

§ 99.66 WHAT ARE THE RESPONSIBILITIES OF THE OFFICE IN THE ENFORCEMENT PROCESS?

(a) The Office reviews the complaint, if any, information submitted by the educational agency or institution, and any other relevant information. The Office may permit the parties to submit further written or oral arguments or information.

(b) Following its investigation, the Office provides to the complainant, if any, and the educational agency or institution a written notice of its findings and the basis for its findings.

(c) If the Office finds that an educational agency or institution has not complied with a provision of the *Act* or this part, it may also find that the failure to comply was based on a policy or practice of the agency or institution. A notice of findings issued under paragraph (b) of this section to an educational agency or institution that has not complied with a provision of the Act or this part:

(1) Includes a statement of the specific steps that the agency or institution must take to comply; and

(2) Provides a reasonable period of time, given all of the circumstances of the case, during which the educational agency or institution may comply voluntarily.

[Authority: 20 u.s.c. 1232g(f)]

§ 99.67 HOW DOES THE SECRETARY ENFORCE DECISIONS?

(a) If an educational agency or institution does not comply during the period of time set under § 99.66(c), the Secretary may take any legally available enforcement action in accordance with the Act, including, but not limited to, the following enforcement actions available in accordance with part E of the *General Education Provisions Act*—

(1) Withhold further payments under any applicable program;

(2) Issue a complaint to compel compliance through a cease-and-desist order; or

(3) Terminate eligibility to receive funding under any applicable program.

(b) If, after an investigation under § 99.66, the Secretary finds that an educational agency or institution has complied voluntarily with the *Act* or this part, the Secretary provides the complainant and the agency or institution written notice of the decision and the basis for the decision.

(Note: 34 C.F.R. Part 78 contains the regulations of the Education Appeal Board.)

[Authority: 20 u.s.c. 1232g(f); 20 u.s.c. 1234]

[Updated January 2009.]

Appendix A to Part 99—Crimes of Violence Definitions

ARSON: Any willful or malicious burning or attempt to burn, with or without intent to defraud, a dwelling house, public building, motor vehicle or aircraft, personal property of another, etc.

ASSAULT OFFENSES: An unlawful attack by one person upon another.

Note: By definition there can be no "attempted" assaults, only "completed" assaults.

(a) *Aggravated Assault.* An unlawful attack by one person upon another for the purpose of inflicting severe or aggravated bodily injury. This type of assault usually is accompanied by the use of a weapon or by means likely to produce death or great bodily harm. (It is not necessary that injury result from an aggravated assault when a gun, knife, or other weapon is used which could and probably would result in serious injury if the crime were successfully completed.)

(b) *Simple Assault.* An unlawful physical attack by one person upon another where neither the offender displays a weapon, nor the victim suffers obvious severe or aggravated bodily injury involving apparent broken bones, loss of teeth, possible internal injury, severe laceration, or loss of consciousness.

(c) *Intimidation.* To unlawfully place another person in reasonable fear of bodily harm through the use of threatening words or other conduct, or both, but without displaying a weapon or subjecting the victim to actual physical attack.

Note: This offense includes stalking.

BURGLARY: The unlawful entry into a building or other structure with the intent to commit a felony or a theft.

CRIMINAL HOMICIDE—MANSLAUGHTER BY NEGLIGENCE: The killing of another person through gross negligence.

CRIMINAL HOMICIDE—MURDER AND NONNEGLIGENT MANSLAUGHTER: The willful (nonnegligent) killing of one human being by another.

DESTRUCTION/DAMAGE/VANDALISM OF PROPERTY: To willfully or maliciously destroy, damage, deface, or otherwise injure real or personal property without the consent of the owner or the person having custody or control of it.

KIDNAPPING/ABDUCTION: The unlawful seizure, transportation, or detention of a person, or any combination of these actions, against his or her will, or of a minor without the consent of his or her custodial parent(s) or legal guardian.

Note: Kidnapping/Abduction includes hostage taking.

ROBBERY: The taking of, or attempting to take, anything of value under confrontational circumstances from the control, custody, or care of a person or persons by force or threat of force or violence or by putting the victim in fear.

Note: Carjackings are robbery offenses where a motor vehicle is taken through force or threat of force.

SEX OFFENSES, FORCIBLE: Any sexual act directed against another person, forcibly or against that person's will, or both; or not forcibly or against the person's will where the victim is incapable of giving consent.

  (a) *Forcible Rape* (Except "Statutory Rape"). The carnal knowledge of a person, forcibly or against that person's will, or both; or not forcibly or against the person's will where the victim is incapable of giving consent because of his or her temporary or permanent mental or physical incapacity (or because of his or her youth).

  (b) *Forcible Sodomy.* Oral or anal sexual intercourse with another person, forcibly or against that person's will, or both; or not forcibly or against the person's will where the victim is incapable of giving consent because of his or her youth or because of his or her temporary or permanent mental or physical incapacity.

  (c) *Sexual Assault with an Object.* To use an object or instrument to unlawfully penetrate, however slightly, the genital or anal opening of the body of another person, forcibly or against that person's will, or both; or not forcibly or against the person's will where the victim is incapable of giving consent because of his or her youth or because of his or her temporary or permanent mental or physical incapacity.

  Note: An "object" or "instrument" is anything used by the offender other than the offender's genitalia. Examples are a finger, bottle, handgun, stick, etc.

(d) *Forcible Fondling.* The touching of the private body parts of another person for the purpose of sexual gratification, forcibly or against that person's will, or both; or not forcibly or against the person's will where the victim is incapable of giving consent because of his or her youth or because of his or her temporary or permanent mental or physical incapacity.

Note: Forcible Fondling includes "Indecent Liberties" and "Child Molesting."

NONFORCIBLE SEX OFFENSES (EXCEPT "PROSTITUTION OFFENSES"): Unlawful, nonforcible sexual intercourse.

(a) *Incest.* Nonforcible sexual intercourse between persons who are related to each other within the degrees wherein marriage is prohibited by law.

(b) *Statutory Rape.* Nonforcible sexual intercourse with a person who is under the statutory age of consent.

[Authority: 20 u.s.c. 1232g(b)(6) and 18 u.s.c. 16]

These regulations were current at the time of publication of this guide. The reader should always check to see if the Department of Education has issued any amendments to these regulations, since publication of this Guide, through the Family Policy Compliance Office (the DOE office that has responsibility for administering FERPA) Web site at: www.ed.gov/policy/gen/guid/fpco/index.html.

◇◇◇◇◇◇◇◇◇◇◇◇◇◇◇◇

Major Points Summarizing the 2009 Regulatory Changes

The following points summarize the major revisions from the 2009 amendments:

◆ Clarifying that the phrase "in attendance" applies to students who may not be physically present in class, such as through online courses.

◆ Clarifying that "biometric records" can be "personally identifiable" and what constitutes "biometric records."

◆ Clarifying that social security numbers, or any part thereof, cannot be designated as directory information.

◆ Clarifying that student identification numbers cannot be designated as directory information, except when they are used as student identifiers to gain access to information from education records, and then, only if in combination with other authentication factors.

◆ Allowing the return of information included in an education record to the originator or purported originator of the information by excluding such transfer of information from the definition of "disclosure."

◆ Clarifying that records pertaining to an individual's previous attendance as a student are "education records" under FERPA, regardless of when they were created or received by the institution.

◆ Summarizing the exceptions that permit postsecondary institutions to disclose information from education records to parents of eligible students.

◆ Clarifying that "personally identifiable information" includes information that alone or in combination, is linked to or linkable to a specific student with reasonable certainty. This replaces the "easily traceable" standard that previously existed within FERPA.

◆ Expanding the "school officials" exception to include contractors, consultants, volunteers, and other outside service providers used by an institution to perform institutional services and functions that it would otherwise perform for itself.

◆ Requiring postsecondary institutions to use "reasonable methods" to ensure that teachers and other school officials (including outside service providers) obtain access to only those education records—paper or electronic—in which they have legitimate educational interests.

◆ Requiring institutions to establish with contractors and other outside service providers expectations about direct control and appropriate use of student data to which they have access.

◆ Allowing a student's previous school to supplement, update, or correct any records it sent during the student's application or transfer period, including disciplinary records.

◆ Requiring a postsecondary institution to enter into a written agreement with an organization that is conducting a study "for or on behalf of" the institution and clarifying that the institution does not have to initiate the study. The agreement should include expectations about appropriate use of student data to which they have access.

◆ Allowing the disclosure of information de-identified through the removal of all "personally identifiable information."

◆ Requiring the use of reasonable methods to identify and authenticate the identity of the student, school officials, parents, and any other parties to whom information from education records is disclosed.

◆ Allowing federal and state officials who receive education records for audit, evaluation, or compliance and enforcement purposes to re-disclose such records in certain circumstances.

◆ Clarifying that, by removing the limitation on redisclosure in §99.33, that releasing the outcome of a disciplinary proceeding to a victim of an alleged crime of violence or a non-forcible sex offense, mandated under the Clery Act, is appropriate under FERPA, and that an institution cannot require such a victim to sign a confidentiality agreement prior to disclosing the outcome of the disciplinary hearing to the victim.

◆ Requiring state or federal officials to whom an institution has disclosed education records to keep a record of redisclosures and provide it to the postsecondary institution upon request.

◆ Revising the conditions under which information from education records may be disclosed in a health or safety emergency, to allow disclosures, including to parents of eligible students, when an institution determines that there is "an articulable and significant threat to the health and safety of the student or other individuals." If such disclosures are made, institutions must record the disclosure and its basis.

◆ Clarifying that directory information may not be disclosed on former students who opted out at their last opportunity to do so while still a student.

◆ Clarifying that opting out of directory information does not provide a student anonymity within a class.

◆ Clarifying that using social security numbers to disclose or confirm directory information is prohibited.

◆ Clarifying that information from education records that has been de-identified can be disclosed by the institution, so long as the information could not reasonably be linked to a specific student.

◆ Clarifying that student identifiable information released to a federal or state educational authority by an institution can be re-disclosed, on behalf of the institution, to another party which could have initially received the information directly from the institution under any of the exceptions in §99.31.

◆ Clarifying and enhancing enforcement provisions of FERPA, pursuant to *Gonzaga University* v. *Doe* 536 U.S. 273 (2002), including that alleged violations brought by someone other than the affected student may be investigated and that a complaint does not have to allege a policy or practice of violating FERPA in order to investigate or find a violation in a specific alleged incident.

◆ Providing additional safeguarding recommendations to help ensure compliance with FERPA.

A copy of the 2009 final regulations are included in Appendix A of this publication. The reader should always check to see if the Department of Education has issued any regulations since publication of this Guide through the

Web page of the Family Policy Compliance Office (FPCO), the office in the Department of Education that has responsibility for administering FERPA, at: www.ed.gov/policy/gen/guid/fpco/index.html *or* www.aacrao.org/compliance/ferpa/.

◇◇◇◇◇◇◇◇◇◇◇◇◇◇◇◇

Model Notification of Rights under FERPA for Postsecondary Institutions

The *Family Educational Rights and Privacy Act* (FERPA) affords students certain rights with respect to their education records. These rights include:

◆ The right to *inspect and review* the student's education records within 45 days of the day the University receives a request for access.

A student should submit to the registrar, dean, head of the academic department, or other appropriate official, a written request that identifies the record(s) the student wishes to inspect. The University official will make arrangements for access and notify the student of the time and place where the records may be inspected. If the records are not maintained by the University official to whom the request was submitted, that official shall advise the student of the correct official to whom the request should be addressed.

◆ The right to request the *amendment* of the student's education records that the student believes are inaccurate, misleading, or otherwise in violation of the student's privacy rights under FERPA.

A student who wishes to ask the University to amend a record should write the University official responsible for the record, clearly identify the part of the record the student wants changed, and specify why it should be changed.

If the University decides not to amend the record as requested, the University will notify the student in writing of the decision and the student's right to a hearing regarding the request for amendment. Additional information regarding the hearing procedures will be provided to the student when notified of the right to a hearing.

◆ The right to provide *written consent* before the University discloses personally identifiable information from the student's education records, except to the extent that FERPA authorizes disclosure without consent.

The University discloses education records without a student's prior written consent under the FERPA exception for disclosure to school officials with legitimate educational interests. A school official is a person employed by the University in an administrative, supervisory, academic or research, or support staff position (including law enforcement unit personnel and health staff); a person or company with whom the University has contracted as its agent to provide a service instead of using University employees or officials (such as an attorney, auditor, or collection agent); a person serving on the Board of Trustees; or a student serving on an official committee, such as a disciplinary or grievance committee, or assisting another school official in performing his or her tasks.

A school official has a legitimate educational interest if the official needs to review an education record in order to fulfill his or her professional responsibilities for the University.

[*Optional*] Upon request, the University also discloses education records without consent to officials of another school in which a student seeks or intends to enroll. [NOTE TO UNIVERSITY: FERPA requires an institution to make a reasonable attempt to notify each student of these disclosures unless the institution states in its annual notification that it intends to forward records on request.]

◆ The right to *file a complaint* with the U.S. Department of Education concerning alleged failures by the University to comply with the requirements of FERPA. The name and address of the Office that administers FERPA is:

Family Policy Compliance Office
U.S. Department of Education
400 Maryland Avenue, SW
Washington, DC 20202-5901

[*Note*: In addition, an institution may want to include its directory infor-mation public notice, as required by § 99.37 of the regulations, with its an-nual notification of rights under FERPA.]

Available for download at: www2.ed.gov/policy/gen/guid/fpco/ferpa/ps-officials.html.

FPCO Guidance Brochure for Colleges[1]

Balancing Student Privacy and School Safety: A Guide to the Family Educational Rights and Privacy Act for Colleges and Universities

Postsecondary officials are regularly asked to balance the interests of safety and privacy for individual students. While the *Family Educational Rights and Privacy Act* (FERPA) generally requires institutions to ask for written consent before disclosing a student's personally identifiable information, it also allows colleges and universities to take key steps to maintain campus safety. Understanding the law empowers school officials to act decisively and quickly when issues arise.

HEALTH OR SAFETY EMERGENCY

In an emergency, FERPA permits school officials to disclose without student consent education records, including personally identifiable information from those records, to protect the health or safety of students or other individuals. At such times, records and information may be released to appropriate parties such as law enforcement officials, public health officials, and trained medical personnel. See 34 C.F.R. 99.31 (a)(10) and 99.36. This exception to FERPA's general consent rule is limited to the period of the emergency and generally does not allow for a blanket release of personally identifiable

---

[1] Available for download in brochure form at <www2.ed.gov/policy/gen/guid/fpco/brochures/elsec.html>.

information from a student's education records. In addition, the Department interprets FERPA to permit institutions to disclose information from education records to parents if a health or safety emergency involves their son or daughter.

DISCIPLINARY RECORDS

While student disciplinary records are protected as education records under FERPA, there are certain circumstances in which disciplinary records may be disclosed without the student's consent. A postsecondary institution may disclose to an alleged victim of any crime of violence or non-forcible sex offense the final results of a disciplinary proceeding conducted by the institution against the alleged perpetrator of that crime, regardless of whether the institution concluded a violation was committed. An institution may disclose to anyone—not just the victim—the final results of a disciplinary proceeding, if it determines that the student is an alleged perpetrator of a crime of violence or non-forcible sex offense, and with respect to the allegation made against him or her, the student has committed a violation of the institution's rules or policies. *See* 34 C.F.R. 99.31 (a)(13) and (14).

THE CLERY ACT

The *Jeanne Clery Disclosure of Campus Security Policy and Campus Crime Statistics Act* requires postsecondary institutions to provide timely warnings of crimes that represent a threat to the safety of students or employees and to make public their campus security policies. It also requires that crime data be collected, reported and disseminated to the campus community and to the Department annually. The *Clery Act* is intended to provide students and their families with accurate, complete and timely information about safety on campuses so that they can make informed decisions. Such disclosures are permitted under FERPA. The following Web site provides more information about these and other provisions about campus safety: www.ed.gov/admins/lead/safety/campus.html.

LAW ENFORCEMENT UNIT RECORDS

Many colleges and universities have their own law enforcement units to monitor safety and security in and around campus. Institutions that do not have specific law enforcement units may designate a particular office or school official to be responsible for referring potential or alleged violations of law to local police authorities. Investigative reports and other records created and maintained by these law enforcement units are not considered education records subject to FERPA. Accordingly, institutions may disclose information from law enforcement unit records to anyone, including outside law enforcement authorities, without student consent. *See* 34 C.F.R. 99.8.

While an institution has flexibility in deciding how to carry out safety functions, it must also indicate in its policy or in information provided to students which office or school official serves as the college or university's "law enforcement unit." (The institution's notification to students of their rights under FERPA can include this designation. As an example, the Department has posted a model notification on its Web site at http://www.ed.gov/policy/gen/guid/fpco/ferpa/ps-officials.html.)

Law enforcement unit officials who are employed by the college or university should be designated in the institution's FERPA notification as "school officials" with a "legitimate educational interest." As such, they may be given access to personally identifiable information from students' education records. The institution's law enforcement unit officials must protect the privacy of education records it receives and may disclose them only in compliance with FERPA. For the reason, it is advisable that law enforcement unit records be maintained separately from education records.

DISCLOSURE TO PARENTS

When a student turns 18 years old or enters a postsecondary institution at any age, all rights afforded to parents under FERPA transfer to the student. However, FERPA also provides ways in which schools may share information with parents without the student's consent. For example:

◆ Schools may disclose education records to parents if the student is a dependent for income tax purposes.

◆ Schools may disclose education records to parents if a health or safety emergency involves their son or daughter.

◆ Schools may inform parents if the student who is under age 21 has violated any law or its policy concerning the use or possession of alcohol or a controlled substance.

◆ A school official may generally share with a parent information that is based on that official's personal knowledge or observation of the student.

FERPA AND STUDENT HEALTH INFORMATION

Postsecondary institutions that provide health or medical services to students may share student medical treatment records with parents under the circumstances described above. While these records may otherwise be governed by the *Health Insurance Portability and Accountability Act of 1996* (HIPAA), the HIPAA Privacy Rule excludes student medical treatment records and other records protected by FERPA. The Department plans to issue further guidance on the interplay between FERPA and HIPAA.

FERPA AND STUDENT AND EXCHANGE VISITOR INFORMATION SYSTEM (SEVIS)

FERPA permits institutions to comply with information requests from the Department of Homeland Security (DHS) and its Immigration and Customs Enforcement Bureau (ICE) in order to comply with the requirements of SEVIS. Officials who have specific questions about this and other matters involving international students should contact the U.S. Department of Education's Family Policy Compliance Office.

TRANSFER OF EDUCATION RECORDS

Finally, FERPA permits school officials to disclose any and all education records, including disciplinary records, to another institution at which the student seeks or intends to enroll. While student consent is not required for transferring education records, the institution's annual FERPA notification should indicate that such disclosures are made. In the absence of information about disclosures in the annual FERPA notification, school officials must make a reasonable attempt to notify the student about the disclosure, unless the student initiates the disclosure. Additionally, upon request, the institution must provide a copy of the information disclosed and an opportunity for a hearing. *See* 34 C.F.R. 99.31(a)(2) and 99.34(a).

CONTACT INFORMATION

For further information about FERPA, please contact the Family Policy Compliance Office or visit its Web site.

Family Policy Compliance Office
U.S. Department of Education
400 Maryland Ave., S.W.
Washington, DC 20202-5901
202-260-3887

For quick, informal responses to routine questions about FERPA, school officials may email the Family Policy compliance Office at ferpa@ed.gov.

For inquiries about FERPA compliance training, contact ferpa.client@ed.gov.

Additional information and guidance may be found at FPCO's Web site at: http://www.ed.gov/policy/gen/guid/fpco/index.html.

∞∞∞∞∞∞∞∞∞∞∞∞∞∞

True/False Quiz & Answer Key

The following tool might be used as a self-test to measure your familiarity/ comfort level with FERPA.

Answers to this quiz can be found at the end of this appendix (on page 93).

1. ___ "Education records" include only those records contained in a student's permanent file.

2. ___ Students must be given the opportunity to inspect and review their education records within 10 days of a request.

3. ___ Faculty has the right to inspect and review the education records of any student.

4. ___ If a student discloses in an open forum that he has been suspended and that he feels the suspension is unwarranted, the school may infer that he has given implied consent for openly discussing the issue.

5. ___ An adviser does not have to allow a student to inspect and review her personal notes about the student that are held in a file in the desk of the adviser's office.

6. ___ The institution doesn't need to provide access to the educational records of a student to a non-custodial parent if the custodial parent

submits a notarized statement that he or she does not consent to the disclosure.

7. ___ A school does not have to send education records to another school in which a student seeks or intends to enroll if the student has an outstanding balance to the current institution.

8. ___ A student has the right to inspect and review an essay submitted by the student, even if the teacher does not intend to return it to the student or to permanently maintain it.

9. ___ Health records, maintained at the student health center, are education records, subject to FERPA.

10. ___ A college newspaper has the right of access to detailed information about disciplinary hearings for students at the institution.

11. ___ A state institution in Ohio must respond to a subpoena received from the Supreme Court of California.

12. ___ An institution should provide data to an engineering firm which asks for a list of all the College of Engineering students who are in the top 10 percent of the senior class.

13. ___ Tom Faculty has posted the grades of all the students in his class on the wall outside his office. This is a violation of FERPA.

14. ___ Sally Student, who is not a dependent student, has been found in violation of the university's residence halls' alcohol policies. Her hall director could contact her parents to discuss the violation without her permission.

15. ___ Admissions records are "education records," therefore covered under FERPA.

16. ___ A student's social security number (SSN) could be verified to a caller who received a document with the student's SSN on it.

17. ___ Ralph Student feels that his college records have been released inappropriately. Ralph can use FERPA to bring a suit against the college.

18. ___ Tom Terrific graduated from State University several years ago. He has been very involved as an alumnus. A journalism student wants to write a story about his involvement at the university, both as a student and as an alumnus. The university should release only his alumni information.

19. ___ Using the institutional student ID number (SIN), Tom Faculty has posted the grades of all the students in his class on the wall outside his office. This is violation of FERPA.

20. ___ "Student recruiting information" under the Solomon Amendment is the same as "directory information" under FERPA.

True/False Quiz Answer Key

Q	A	Notes
1	F	With specific exceptions, "education records" are those maintained by the institution in any format that is identifiable to the student.
2	F	While institutions legally have 45 days to respond, consider whether you prefer and are able to fulfill the request in a more timely fashion, and whether your state open records law identifies a more abbreviated time frame for response.
3	F	All faculty and staff must show a "legitimate educational interest/need to know" within the context of their role to have appropriate access to education records.
4	F	There is no implied consent in FERPA, so you need to follow regular guidelines for releasing this student record information.
5	T	"Sole possession" records are an exception to the definition of "education records," and are therefore not accessible by the student.
6	F	If the student is legally financially dependent on either parent, then either parent can submit a request to access the student's record. If the institution would provide access for one parent, it may do so for either parent.
7	T	While the institution must provide access to the student, it is not required to do so for any third party.
8	T	So long as the record currently exists, it would be part of the student's "education record" and the student has the right to access it.
9	F	Medical treatment records are not covered by FERPA, so long as they are shared only with other medical service providers.
10	F	If the student is found in violation of the institution's conduct code related to a "crime of violence," then the student's name, violation and result of the disciplinary hearing are public information—releasable to anyone. Detailed disciplinary records are never public information, and the names of any victims or witnesses cannot be disclosed without consent.
11	F	A state court has legal jurisdiction only within that state. However, it is permissible for the institution in Ohio to respond to the California subpoena as a matter of professional courtesy. All the FERPA requirements regarding responding to subpoenas must be followed.

T=True, F=False, D=Depends

Q	A	Notes
12	F	There are three issues here. First, grades and GPAs can never be directory information. Academic honors (e.g., Dean' s List) can be directory information if the school has so designated academic honors to fall in that category. The question of top 10% of grades falls into a somewhat gray area, since it does not directly provide access to grade information for an individual student, but also does not meet the definition of directory information. In fact, it may come close to identifying grade information. Our recommendation is that schools not release the names of students in a top category of grades if that category is not designated as an academic honor in directory information.
13	D	It depends on HOW he posted the grades. If by name, Student ID Number, SSN (or part thereof), or something that can be fairly easily interpreted by a third party, then "yes," it's a violation. However, if the grades were posted by some "code" known only by the student and instructor, then that's OK.
14	T	This is true for any student under the age of 21—regardless of whether or not the student is financially dependent on his or her parent. Note that some state laws prohibit sharing this information without permission.
15	D	If the student is not yet "in attendance," then records related to the admission would generally not be an "education record." This is also true if the student is never admitted. However, if admitted and enrolled, all admissions records the institution continues to maintain become education records. It is also important that institutions familiarize themselves with state law and when education records start under those provisions since some begin once an institution begins creating a record.
16	F	A student's social security number can never be directory information, and therefore cannot be disclosed or even confirmed as public information.
17	F	There is no private cause of action under FERPA. This issue was confirmed by the U.S. Supreme Court in Gonzaga University v. John Doe, a 2002 decision. The student might want to pursue action under a Common Law or state law remedy, such as libel or slander.
18	F	The 2009 regulations clarified that records created after the student was enrolled are considered Alumni Records and are generally open to the public because they are not "education records" under FERPA. Since this is a state school, the state's open records law may apply if FERPA does not. Unless the student has a "No Release" on his record, you could also release directory information about Tom from when he was a student.
19	T	Posting grades in any personally identifiable format, such as with a name, SSN or SIN, would be a violation under FERPA.
20	F	"Student Recruiting Information" is a set of data defined within the Solomon Amendment. "Directory information" is a set of data defined by each institution. While there MAY be substantial overlap among the data items at any specific institution, they are not the same.

T=True, F=False, D=Depends